Arise and Call

Her Blessed

—— A Daughter's Memoir ——

C. D. Collins

THE HOLY BIBLE, NEW INTERNATIONAL VERSION®, NIV® Copyright © 1973, 1978, 1984, 2011 by Biblica, Inc.® Used by permission. All rights reserved worldwide.

This book is a work of non-fiction. Unless otherwise noted, the author and the publisher make no explicit guarantees as to the accuracy of the information contained in this book and, in some cases, names of people and places have been altered to protect their privacy.

ISBN: 978-1-4834-6603-3 (sc)
ISBN: 978-1-4834-6604-0 (hc)
ISBN: 978-1-4834-6602-6 (e)

Library of Congress Control Number: 2017902838

Because of the dynamic nature of the Internet, any web addresses or links contained in this book may have changed since publication and may no longer be valid. The views expressed in this work are solely those of the author and do not necessarily reflect the views of the publisher, and the publisher hereby disclaims any responsibility for them.

Any people depicted in stock imagery provided by Thinkstock are models, and such images are being used for illustrative purposes only. Certain stock imagery © Thinkstock.

Lulu Publishing Services rev. date: 03/09/2017

Preface

This is a collection of memories: five decades worth of memories of being Kakki's daughter and only child. When I cast back for those memories of my mom, the ones that surface the quickest are the ones of when we are laughing or playing together. She was so much fun, and was unquestionably the most profound influence on my life. Her love for me was unconditional, and like most mothers she would have sacrificed her life for mine without hesitation. Her childhood was challenging, growing up during the Great Depression as the eldest of four, but she knew that the mother-child relationship was fundamental and worked hard at getting it right. She balanced love with discipline and punishment with praise; and she knew precisely when to move from manager, handling every detail of my life and making all of the decisions, to counselor, recognizing that I was becoming a young adult and that it was critical for her role to change to that of trusted friend and advisor.

Like all of us, she was far from perfect. She possessed a first-rate temper, giving a face to the term road-rage long before it became fashionable; she had a tendency to want to live above our means, which put undue pressure on my father as chief breadwinner; and she displayed a touch of hypochondria—but more about that later.

I have put my memories on paper for two reasons. The most important reason is to honor a wonderful human being who also happened to be my beloved mother. The other reason is to share an example. I have read stories of people who, for various reasons, had difficult relationships with their mothers. Some people whom I actually know tried time and again to "climb the hill" for their mothers' affection and approval, and time and again they were repelled for one reason or another. I believe that people can function at very high levels in spite of the absence of a nurturing mother-child relationship, but I think it takes a tremendous amount of work on their part, and time—precious time.

What a compliment to my mother if someone were to read this and find in our story some examples worth following as she raises her own children. And for those mothers with adult children who think that it is too late, I tell you it is never too late. Allow that child, even if he or she is grown, to "climb the hill." You and they will be forever changed.

Introduction

While the Preface of this book is intended to provide the reader with the "why," giving the compelling reasons for capturing my mother's life in a memoir, this Introduction is designed to provide the reader with the "how."

This memoir is basically laid out chronologically from my birth to her death. Obviously, her life's experiences before I was born were told to me, either by her or a family member or a friend. There was also a period of time when I was fully engaged in a career several hours away that caused her day-to-day activities to basically be unknown to me. I have counted on the recollections of her dear friends and family to paint a picture of her life during that time.

Even though the chronology is the backbone of the story, many times I have departed from the backbone, out onto the tip of one of the vertebrae, so to speak, in order to unfurl details about a characteristic, an experience, or a life lesson relevant to her memory. The unfurling often swings out away from the backbone decades into the future, and sometimes reverts decades into the past, but always makes the turn, in due time, and circles back to the basic chronology from my birth to her death.

I found this narrative style quite handy. There were times when I needed to provide my perceptions for her idiosyncrasies and there were times when aspects of her character were more completely illustrated by stories that didn't follow the strict timing of the chronology. But, most importantly, this narrative style allowed me to provide pertinent details for the countless ways in which she influenced me and shaped my life for the better. If you find yourself in one of these loops, rest assured you will soon be returned.

Finally, I have chosen to change the names of the vast majority of non-family members in an effort to protect their privacy. Some details regarding specific places have also been modified for the same reason.

However, I have not modified any details or specifics about my mother's character or her life. The writing is, after all, a tribute to her genuine, flawed, magnificent self. I hope you enjoy reading it as much as I have enjoyed writing it.

Earth's crammed with heaven, and every common bush afire with God;
But only he who sees, takes off his shoes,
The rest sit 'round it, and pluck blackberries...

Elizabeth Barrett Browning
Aurora Leigh

For Mom, may she rest in peace

She speaks with wisdom, and faithful instruction is on her tongue.
Her children arise and call her blessed.

Proverbs 31: 26, 28 (NIV)

1

We met for the first time on January 16, 1959, at about 7:30 in the evening after more than seventeen hours of labor. I was a big girl, eight pounds, thirteen ounces, and twenty-two inches long, with a head full of black hair. My mother had actually wished for a boy, and if I had been a boy, my name would have been Kirk Allen—Allen after my father, and Kirk after Kirk Douglas, the actor, whom my father resembled back then, minus the cleft in the chin. My father, however, had wanted a little girl and had picked out the name Cheryl Diane. Strangely enough, the name Cheryl came from the newspaper months earlier when Cheryl Crane, daughter of Lana Turner, made headlines by stabbing her mother's abusive boyfriend in an effort to protect her mother. I have no idea where Diane came from, but likely a less infamous source.

I always delighted in the description my mother would share about my father's reaction to my birth. Mom said she had never seen a happier man. She recalled looking at him sideways from her gurney and seeing his young face and lanky body taking giant bouncing steps toward her, clapping his hands, and saying, "She's beautiful, just beautiful! I couldn't have taken paper and pencil and drawn her more perfect." Mom remembered her own reaction as complete awe of the little body in her arms and being at a total loss for words. She recounted, "I ended up saying, 'Well, hello there.'"

Years later, after learning about the seventeen hours of labor and seeing a few television shows dramatizing the birth of a child, I actually apologized to my mother for putting her through that. She responded simply that she wouldn't trade anything for me—music to my ears. I also stayed in there eleven days longer than I was supposed to—accounting for, I suspect, my hefty birth weight and length. I guess I just wasn't ready to leave her, a theme that would be repeated two more times over the next eighteen years.

I was born in Killeen, Texas, where my father was an MP stationed at Killeen Base. Killeen Base was an atomic weapons storage facility back in 1959, one of seven located in five different states and the only one operated by the US Army. My parents lived in one side of a small duplex in Copperas Cove. Legend has it that my comedic father referred to it as Copper-Ass Cove. When my dad was off duty from the base, he worked at a gas station owned by a local oil company. The owner of the oil company, my dad's boss, and his wife lived in the other side of the duplex.

From all accounts, my mom enjoyed her time in Texas. She worked as an operator for the local telephone company, played a lot of cards, and did a lot of fishing. Mom was a "when in Rome" kind of girl and embraced the western culture of Texas with gusto, learning how to tool leather and posing for photos in full cowgirl regalia. I still have those photos that showcase her loveliness—the cowboy hat accentuating her pretty face with the belted pants, cowgirl blouse, and boots showing off her curvy figure and long legs. In photos of my mother in her twenties, I think she looks like a cross between Ava Gardner and Sophia Loren in the sultry, pouty-mouthed black and white photos of the two beauties.

My mom didn't marry until she turned twenty-eight, which in the 1950s was a little long in the tooth. It wasn't for a lack of boyfriends, however. I heard stories about N., the high school boyfriend with the long eyelashes upon which she used to stack toothpicks; and B., the handsome slightly older man whom she was extremely attracted to and dated for a while—until she found out he was married. She then "dropped him like a hot potato." She also dated a preacher who puzzled her with his requests that she not wear shorts in his presence. However, when they went swimming, a bathing suit was acceptable. There was also a young man whose name I cannot recall who apparently could not resist the urge to walk over and meet her while she gave the appearance of sketching him. Mom was attracted to the tall, dark, handsome type, which makes it rather a mystery how she and my father, twenty years old when they married and cute rather than handsome, ever got together. He was medium height, light-skinned, blond and blue-eyed. He was extremely charming, however, and I can just imagine that charm in action, along with the toothy grin, as the country boy tried to get the lovely city girl's attention while he serviced her car, filling it with gasoline and cleaning the windshield. Whatever he did, it worked; and after a short engagement, Floyd Allen Collins and Kathryn Virginia Adams, a.k.a. Kakki, were married in Birmingham, Alabama, on March 5, 1955, in my maternal grandmother's house on Border Street.

Their marriage was probably ill-fated from the start. Age differences between spouses can often present difficulties, especially when the age difference is eight years and the wife is the elder. Furthermore, my father often behaved younger than his years and my mother was more mature than hers, which made the perceptional age gap even wider. My parents fought a lot and usually over money. But at least the fighting was only verbal, never physical. They were just so very different. My father, a certified extrovert, was the life of any party and could tell a joke or a funny story like nobody's business. Occasionally, my mother would be the butt of those jokes, and I remember her always handling the hard teasing with much more grace than I felt like affording him. He was flirtatious and childish and delighted in being the center of attention. He was loved by hundreds of people and could always make them laugh. My mother, on the other hand, was more stoic and an introvert, preferring the company of a few intimate friends to a gathering of many acquaintances.

Twenty-eight years into their marriage, my father was moved to action when his secret affections for another woman came to light. The web of deceit my father had woven had finally entangled him, and now trapped, he was forced to come clean. My mother was devastated and shared with me that she could have lost him to death easier than losing him to another woman. I was twenty-four years old and married at the time, and although I was deeply saddened by my mother's heartbreak and furious with my father for hurting her, I actually viewed their divorce with relief. I saw it as an opportunity for her to finally escape the disrespectful treatment by the impish little boy whom I deemed as far too wounded to provide her with a true partnership.

As for my father, I guess he really loved my mother and perhaps just had difficulty showing it. Lest the reader of this chronicle think otherwise, I remain extremely proud to have been his daughter. His behavior toward my mother was a source of significant disappointment for me over the years, but it didn't lessen my love for him.

After my mother's death in May 2010 and my father's death in September of the same year, my stepmother, a woman whom I came to love, told me that I would likely never know how deeply my mother's death had affected my father. His actions twenty-seven years earlier, however, had taken her to a brink, but her inner strength and faith pulled her back.

My mother's strength was one of her most beautiful characteristics, and I saw it on full display many times during our years together. There were three events, however, that stand out in my memory. The first and foremost was, of course, my father's deception. It took her several years to recover, and if I had been wiser, I would have advised counseling for her grief. She managed the process on her own, however, oddly enough by listening to the country music station at night and, true to form, by staying closely connected to her church. Her closest friends and I worried about the country music therapy, wondering how someone could possibly heal by listening to music that thematically often included lyrics of sadness and loss and relationships gone bad. Maybe it comforted her to know she wasn't the only one, as lyricists often write from their own experiences. Whatever it was, slowly but surely she began to emerge from her dark place.

During those difficult months, my mother certainly had many opportunities to act out, cause scenes, or make my father's life miserable, but she never did. Only one word is needed to describe my mother's public behavior during and following the divorce: *class*. I remember being very proud of her during this extremely difficult period of her life.

The second event was the death of her uncle Huey. Huey, a.k.a. Preacher, was my grandmother's brother and battled alcoholism for most of his adult life. In April 1965 at the age of fifty-three, he drowned in his own vomitus in the bathtub of a rundown boardinghouse on the seedier side of Birmingham. My mother was the one the family called upon to go and identify his body. I remember being left in the car and watching as my parents threaded their way through parked police cars and then went inside the old house. Moments later, I recall seeing my father escorting my crying mother back down the steps of the boardinghouse after having identified Uncle Huey's body. Of course, at the time, my parents shared no details whatsoever with me because I was just a child; but years later, Mom told me the story in more detail. I remember thinking, *Wow, that took a lot of emotional strength.*

The third event involved yet another death in our family, but this one was much more difficult. My first-cousin Steve, age twenty-eight, my mother's nephew and son of her only brother, Bill, was killed in an industrial accident in the Louisiana bayou in April 1982. His death was very sudden and so violent that the casket at the funeral remained closed. I was twenty-three years old when Steve was killed and actually accompanied my mother to the home of Aunt Wilma and Uncle Bill to deliver the news. With visible empathy and compassionate directness, she told them of Steve's demise. I watched her in awe and reverence and then took her lead as we gave my aunt and uncle physical and emotional space to absorb the shock, waiting in the wings in case we were needed. It was a beautiful lesson for me in human kindness, respect, and empathy; and I clearly remember thinking to myself, *Where did she learn how to do that?*

My mother's ability to maintain her poise and her emotional balance in difficult times made deep and lasting impressions on me. She did not approach these challenges with trepidation but rather from a sense of duty; a sense that this or that "must be done." I am certain that, if she were alive today and presented with such a compliment, she would credit her Christian beliefs and her faith in God. But I also believe she would credit her own mother. Today, as both my grandmother and my mother are citizens of heaven, where forgiveness, understanding, and love are perfected, I believe they bask in the glow of each other. The earthly relationship, however, was delicate and somewhat of a mystery to me.

5

In the writing of this memoir, facets of their relationship were perhaps made clearer, just as pondering and recording one's thoughts and feelings on any situation can often provide clarity. I have no doubt that my grandmother loved my mother. I recall my mother telling a wonderful story about my grandmother riding to Mom's rescue when her youngest sibling, my aunt Gail, innocently invited one of my mother's boyfriends, the preacher, as luck would have it, to a picnic—a picnic that neither my mother nor my grandmother knew anything about. When my mother became aware of the spurious invitation, she was near panic as no plans whatsoever had been laid. My grandmother took the surprise in easy stride, told Mom not to worry a whit, and pulled together a picnic fit for a king (or at least a boyfriend) consisting of fried chicken, home-made potato salad, and all the trimmings. My young aunt completed the surprise package by hiding in the back seat as my mother and the preacher drove away for their picnic, reappearing in time to enjoy the food and the company.

Despite such fond remembrances, however, my mother's general interpretation of her mother's affection was that my grandmother doled out her love in measure with the child's lovability. Right or wrong, my mother sensed a minimized affection from my grandmother and fought down feelings of inadequacy. That interpretation of being "less loved" was an open wound that my mother carried for her entire life. It did not affect her love for her siblings, particularly for her youngest sibling, or her mother for that matter, but I believe it lead to a mild case of hypochondria. Migraine headaches, stomach upsets, and the like were common occurrences for my mother; and when I became an adult I saw the illnesses as perhaps having been spawned by a subconscious need for attention that she interpreted as having been denied her in her formative years.

When I became an adult, my mother and I discussed her relationship with my grandmother many times. I was honored that she would confide such deep and personal feelings with me; and at first, I will admit, I felt extremely protective of my mother and seeds of anger and disappointment were unwittingly planted in my heart toward my grandmother. My mother however recognized the wonderful relationship I had with my grandmother and simply would not allow those seeds to grow. I think it was just therapeutic for her to talk about the subject, and in truth, I believe she enjoyed mine and my grandmother's relationship vicariously. Mom was self-aware and knew that her stoicism and her infamous temper probably made her difficult to be around from time to time and caused my grandmother to walk on eggshells. She also was keenly attuned to how difficult it must have been to raise four children during the Depression and to loose your husband and love of your life at age forty-three.

As for me, I choose to believe that my grandmother recognized the unique inner strength of her eldest child, admired it, and counted on it. Perhaps, as she struggled, along with my grandfather, to raise their four children (the first two only eighteen months apart), she had to pull back emotionally in order to survive and knew that Mom had the strength of character to make it, no matter what. If that was indeed my grandmother's judgment, then I would have to agree with her. If what they say about apples not falling far from the tree is true, then it is without question that my grandmother did a lot of things right.

My parents spent about eighteen months in Texas; enough time to meet and become friends with another Army couple who would remain fixtures in our lives for decades to come. They were from central Alabama, just like my parents, and both couples found a lot of common ground upon which to forge a friendship. Ms. Nita and my mom quickly became "running buddies," fishing together (although that was really Mom's liking and not Ms. Nita's), playing cards, and checking out the local attractions. My father and Mr. Eugene worked together at Killeen Base and at the gas station; and although they soon became great friends, they were polar opposites in temperament. On one occasion, while Dad and Mr. Eugene were at work, Mom and Ms. Nita decided to drive to Lampasas, Texas, about eighteen miles west of Copperas Cove to do some sightseeing. Much to their dismay, they experienced two flat tires during the trip. Mom, in a minor panic, asked Ms. Nita to please telephone the calm, cool, and collected Mr. Eugene to come rescue them, because she certainly didn't want to have to call my father. Unfortunately, my dad saw Mr. Eugene leaving the base and asked the obvious question. Mr. Eugene innocently afforded the answer and my father, as the story goes, hit the roof.

Years after returning to Alabama, the couple divorced, and Mr. Eugene soon faded from our circle; but Ms. Nita never did and was my mom's longest and most treasured friendship. She is among the most generous people I have ever met and is the person I have tried to emulate regarding that virtue. After my parents' divorce, it was not the least bit unusual for my mother to find a wad of twenties, rolled up and stashed just out of easy sight atop her bedroom dresser, where Ms. Nita would have hidden it while visiting. She has led a very interesting life, full of adventure, entrepreneurial achievement, and a few interesting romances to boot. My mother loved her unconditionally, and Ms. Nita treasured that love.

We spent only about six months in Texas after I was born, and upon my father's honorable discharge from the Army we made our way to Birmingham, Alabama. My parents initially rented a small house around the block from my grandmother's house on Border Street. We lived there for a few months until they found and bought a home in a lower middle class neighborhood called West End, just around the corner from Uncle Bill and Aunt Wilma and their children, Donna and Steve. I adored Aunt Wilma and often stayed with her when my parents' work schedules overlapped. Birmingham and the surrounding area was actually home to the vast majority of my extended family, which was wonderful because I was able to visit and enjoy holidays with grandmothers, cousins, aunts, and uncles for the next several years.

The downside of Birmingham however was the wet winters, which exacerbated the ear, nose, and throat trouble I often experienced as a young child. After my pediatrician conducted some tests and concluded I was allergic to dust, my mother turned her focus on my newly identified enemy and conducted a daily wipe-down of my room with an anti-bacterial cleaning solution. To facilitate the laborious daily task, my room was kept very spartan. There was an iron headboard bed and a small side table, home to the large glass jar that my mother filled with water every night and covered with a large black lid containing a small recess for mentholated ointment. When the vaporizer was plugged in, the penetrating warm vapor would fill my room and make my breathing easier.

Some of my most treasured memories of my mother are of her tending to me when I was ill with some sort of malady, almost always in my ears, nose, or throat. Her gentleness and home remedies were a source of deep comfort—an earache always meant drops, small cotton balls, a heating pad upon which to rest my aching ear, and a soothing back rub to help me go to sleep. If the infection moved to my chest, out would come the ironing board, one of Daddy's soft undershirts, and the Vapor-Rub. First, she would iron the undershirt until it was very warm to the touch; and then she would apply the salve to my little chest, careful to not allow the menthol to chill me, and then quickly lay the warm tee shirt on top. It was a diligent and very loving routine that always made me feel better.

My mother was a natural caretaker and were it not for the death of her father in 1949 when he was only forty-seven, she likely would have finished the nurse's training she was enrolled in at Grady Memorial Hospital in Atlanta, Georgia. My mother was a Daddy's girl and was deeply saddened by the loss of her father; but as the eldest of the four children, and with her brother in the Navy and the second oldest sibling already married and living in Florida, the head of household responsibilities fell naturally to Mom. So, at age twenty-two she stopped her nurse's training and moved back to Birmingham to help care for her mother and her younger sister, my aunt Gail, who was only eleven at the time of their father's death.

I recall my mother's experiences in nurse's training providing a canvas for her illustration of a significant life lesson. To this day, it ranks among the most important lessons I ever learned from her. While studying the obstetrics module, she assisted with many deliveries. She told me that in the early days of her assignments in the maternity ward, she was very empathetic and felt every contraction and every pain experienced by the mothers-to-be. She did her best to soothe them with calm words and encouragement and reminded them they were "almost through it." After several months, however, she noted a transition in her feelings toward the mothers; and although she never spoke her thoughts aloud, she shared with me that she often wanted to say, "Oh, my word! Women have babies everyday! Now hush your whining and PUSH!"

She found this evolution of her feelings, from compassion to insensitivity, very disturbing but realized the unbidden shift was nonetheless entirely natural human behavior. She shared some fundamental insights with me. First, realize that the natural ebb for anyone is toward less sensitivity, less empathy, less understanding, more entitlement; and second, counter that by employing a strong set of personal checks and balances in the form of bluntly honest, true friends, daily devotionals, and self-critique.

Upon her return to Birmingham in 1949, she quickly began looking for employment. Her search ended when she was offered a job as a telephone operator with Southern Bell, headquartered in downtown Birmingham. Her career at Southern Bell spanned the next seventeen and one-half years, including an eighteen-month leave of absence from 1957 to 1959 in order to accompany my father to Texas for his first military assignment following basic training and to have me.

Her career experiences as an operator for Southern Bell were the source of several significant life-lessons for me. One very impactful lesson, and one I carried with me throughout my own career, was her beliefs and corresponding behavior during a labor strike, which had the operators and other employee classifications working for Southern Bell on the picket line. Mom recalled that the strike organizers gave instruction to verbally abuse anyone crossing the line and, further, to make their trek through the front door as difficult as possible. My mother told them that she would carry the sign and walk the picket line but would not treat anyone with disrespect. Her core values simply would not support that type of behavior. She fundamentally believed that the workers not being at their assigned stations should be enough to make the company realize the importance of the positions and would be the strongest bargaining chip available.

To balance the picture of her noble behavior on the picket line, she told me of two times she had broken the rules by listening in on calls she had connected for customers. The first time was to listen to a conversation between Elvis and his mother—understandable; the second turned out to be a far more sinister conversation between police detectives working to solve the kidnapping of a young boy in the Birmingham area. After finding him, deceased and disgraced, the detectives were discussing the details on their phone call. My mother recalled being literally sickened and deeply despaired for the mother and father of the little boy. She shared her profound regret for her actions with me and told me it had taken her years to stop thinking about the crime. She helped me understand that sometimes breaking the rules can appear to be fun, but continuing the practice will always eventually catch up with you, and the price you pay will be significant.

For the entire seven years we lived in Birmingham, both of my parents worked. When Mom was on dayshift at the telephone company, she would drop me off at kindergarten on her way downtown. Almost every morning I would cry a river, anticipating the separation. She assured me she would return for me at the end of the day, and she encouraged me to play and learn and make new friends. In 1965, Tom Jones was on the airwaves singing "What's New Pussycat" and the disc jockey seemed to play that song every morning, about ten minutes before we arrived at the school. The music and the tone of his voice sounded so sad to me; and when he would sing those lyrics, "What's new pussycat, whoa, whoa, whoa, oh," well, it was more than I could bear. The tears would begin to flow and Mom would begin to console. My tears were not really those of a sad child but more the tears of a fearful child, fearful that for some reason she would not return for me. Of course this was completely baseless, but children cannot always talk themselves into a logical reckoning.

Each day, right after lunch, we children would move, single file, up the staircase for a rest period. The upstairs room was packed with evenly spaced little cots. A desk was situated near the top of the stairs so that one of our teachers could watch over us, lest a little escapee try to skip the nap.

I rarely slept. Occasionally, something would grab my attention, like the explosion of tiny pieces of lint that would jump off my socked foot as I wiggled it back and forth, the lint momentarily suspended in a shaft of sunlight that had crept in around the edges of the drawn shades. Mostly however, I occupied myself with visions of my mom, dressed up for work. During this period of adjustment, having to be away from her for hours at a time—and not being in the care of my beloved Aunt

Wilma—she was very patient with me, never got angry over the tears, and kept her promises. Slowly, I began to handle the separation better.

At Christmas time one year, our kindergarten teachers decided we would each have a gift under our enormous school tree, and the day before Christmas break the teachers would hand out our gifts, and we would all open them at the same time. The catch was our parents were to choose the gift, wrap it, and send it to school with us without us knowing what it was. I dutifully and excitedly took the instructions home. My father announced that he had an idea for a gift and would bring it home so Mom could wrap it.

My father worked as an aircraft mechanic for a natural gas company, also headquartered in Birmingham, that had a fleet of corporate planes. It was this company's custom to airdrop little parachutes attached to a red nylon mesh stocking filled with small plastic toys and Christmas edibles into the backyards of the children of company executives. My father had access to this stash of goodies and brought home a plastic set of cockpit earphones and a little hula dancer for my kindergarten present. My mother took one look at the hula dancer and became rather animated. I stepped into the den to see what was going on and witnessed the discussion about the inappropriateness of one's daughter unwrapping a hula dancer at the kindergarten Christmas celebration, especially since she had on only the skirt and no top to cover her ample bosom, albeit plastic. All I could say was, "I'm not suppose to see! I'm not suppose to see!" trying desperately to get my parents to adhere to the rules of the gift giving. In the end, I unwrapped a set of plastic cockpit earphones at the kindergarten party and pretended to be both surprised and thrilled. Later that same Christmas season, I, too, was the recipient of one of the airdrops. It was very exciting seeing the little gray parachute floating gently through the sky and landing in my backyard. When I gathered it up from the ground, all memory of the surprise gift that was not a surprise dissolved away.

Our house in Birmingham was a typical home for the area and featured a driveway perpendicular to the street and leading to a carport on one side of the house. At the back of the carport stood a detached utility room, which held the washing machine. One day while I was playing outside, a car pulled up at the end of our driveway and stopped in the street. I remember a man wearing a hat in the driver's seat, looking at me and speaking to me. I could not understand what he was saying, so I walked a little closer. Again he spoke, and again it was too soft for me to hear, so I edged closer still. My next awareness was the sound of my mother calling my name and the sight of her standing, like a momma grizzly bear, in the open door of the utility room with some clothes draped over her arm, prepared to risk life and limb in the protection of her cub. The car screeched forward and roared out of sight. Was he up to no good? God only knows, but that experience was my first clear memory of the abiding, watchful presence of my mother.

I have often wondered if her observation of my behavior that day was not the first in a series of observations she had made of me over the years that led her to the conclusion that it was my natural bent to trust—and to trust to the point where I was vulnerable to people looking to take advantage and not having my best interests at heart. My propensity worried her no end. Over our years together, I cannot count the number of times my mother told me, in gentle yet firm words, "Cheri, you are too trusting."

Just days after her death in May 2010, I dreamt of a small band of attractive young people, male and female, traveling by rowboat and landing on the shore of my lake home. They walked together up the hill to my house and knocked on the front door. When I answered the door they all smiled at me, made brief eye contact, and spoke not one word. Then, without invitation and despite my mild protestations, they just walked past me and into the living room. They began to remove things, carrying them right out the front door; and despite my confusion and questions, I was unable to stop them. When I awoke the next morning, I thought immediately of my mother's persistent warning and decided she had likely authored that dream story to serve as a final reminder of her wise counsel, "Honey, be gentle as a lamb, but cautious as a serpent."

My mom was also a great believer in karma. I'm not sure she would have used that particular word, but she most definitely believed that the yardstick we used to measure others would one day be used to measure us. I heard her tell the story of our experience at the Alabama State Fair many times, and as I aged I began to understand the subtleties of the story. She began by telling the listener how she had remarked, many times, that people who lost their children at the fair, wanted to loose them—until the day she lost me. She recounted the panic she felt when she looked down at her side and did not see me. Turning in circles, calling my name, and trying desperately to stay calm, she described the process of breathing deeply, composing herself, and strategizing. "I must think like Cheri would think," she said to herself. She recalled my intense reluctance to leave the ponies just minutes before and thought perhaps I had gone back there. She made her way through the crowd, making an effort not to lose her composure, and sure enough, there I was, leaning on the little rope watching the tiny horses walk round in circles. With me then in sight, she looked for the teaching moment. She decided she would follow me and see what I would do. Soon, she saw me begin to look up into the adult faces of the crowd as I walked and reasoned that I was beginning to look for her. Then, she recounted, without explanation I wheeled around and looked up into her face and asked indignantly, "Momma, where have you been?" At this point, listeners to her story always dissolved into giggles at the comical audacity of the child, the story ending well, no harm done. The subtlety of the story was the valuable lesson that we seem to spend our lives learning and re-learning—what goes around, comes around.

My assignment for kindergarten graduation was memorizing and then reciting the Twenty-Third Psalm at our commencement services. There was no shortage of Bibles in my home, so I found one, looked up the Psalm, and set out to memorize it. When I thought I had it, I walked into the kitchen one evening where Mom was preparing our dinner and asked her to listen. She answered kindly that of course she would, but with the multi-tasking genius of all mothers, she gave me an ear while keeping an eye on dinner preparations. I went through the passage. When I finished, I waited, rather breathlessly, for her response. I recall her taking the pot off the burner and slowly turning to look at me as if a small alien had just landed in her kitchen. She was literally dumbstruck. When she found her voice, she told me what a wonderful job I had done. I think that was the precise moment in my life when I subconsciously became addicted to doing things that brought my mother joy, and conversely avoiding actions that would bring her unhappiness.

Memorizing the words to the Twenty-Third Psalm was a manageable challenge, but I definitely needed her help with interpretation. For example, if the Lord was so good, why would I not want Him? I reasoned perhaps it was because he *made* me lie down. Mom explained that first verse to mean that the Lord is my Shepard, that I will not lack for anything I need, and that green pastures are wonderful to lie down on. I also wasn't sure about pouring the oil over my head; that sounded messy and wasteful. Mom explained that it wasn't a lot and would make my hair smell really nice. And then "surely goodness and mercy" came out more like the three sisters, Shirley, Goodness, and Mercy. Mom explained it this way—certainly good things and understanding would follow me all the days of my life.

I recall the commencement service, the little white cap and gown, the black patent leather shoes with the white turned down socks with lace on the edges, and the click-click of my heels as I crossed the wooden stage. The audience was in shadow but I found and locked in on my parents' gray faces. I recited. Afterward, Mom recounted the story to family and friends. She told of the hush that fell across the audience as I walked onto the stage alone, the ability to hear a pin drop during the recital, and the collective intake of breath at the end. It was times like those, when my parents expressed obvious delight, that infused me with eagerness to please them again and again. My parents often joked that perhaps I had been switched at birth, neither of them able to understand how two "C" students had given birth to an "A" student.

The years we spent in Birmingham, the last half of 1959 through 1966, were tense with racial difficulties, and I remember my parents basically disagreeing on the desired outcome. My father was not a violent man and would never have physically harmed anyone, regardless of their race, but he clearly believed in the superiority of the white race and hoped all of that civil rights rhetoric would eventually subside. My mother, on the other hand, was completely baffled as to why a black person had to use a different entrance into a restaurant or a different bathroom. Working in downtown Birmingham, she occasionally used public transportation, and would not hesitate to rise from her seat in the "whites only" section and offer it to an elderly or infirm black man or woman. As a convinced Christian, she believed the Creator had unconditional love for all of His creation and would certainly desire that everyone be treated the same. Her beliefs and behaviors during this time of turmoil in the deep South were a shining example for me and became the foundation for my own beliefs regarding racial equality.

My parents' political leanings were yet another difference in their personalities. Dad usually voted straight Republican and Mom usually voted her conscience, sometimes Democratic, sometimes Republican. My father could more easily accept the axiom about the end justifying the means, whereas my mother rarely could—it mattered to her how you got there. Mom joked that she didn't know why she and Daddy even bothered to vote because they usually cancelled each other out.

Birmingham was also the backdrop for my introduction to organized religion and the Christian faith. My parents were very active in a local church, and I remember us faithfully attending the various services held on Sundays and on Wednesday nights. My mother was a Sunday School teacher and my father was a deacon and a tenor in the choir. As in most churches, the young children garner a lot of attention and our church was no exception. Mom would dress me to the nines in pantaloons and crisp little dresses along with my lacy socks and black patent leather shoes; my "outfits" always seemed to be a hit with the adults at the church. I have fairly clear memories of the oohs and ahhs as I walked hand in hand with my mother into or out of the sanctuary.

For Easter services, Mom and I both would have new dresses and Dad, depending on the budget, might have a new suit, but always at least a new shirt and tie. My mom was a bit of a fashionista, and standing five feet eight inches in her bare feet and with her striking good looks and lovely figure she was quite the head turner, especially when decked out in hose and heels and a flattering frock.

Adams family lore has it that at least one of my mother's great-great grandmothers was full-blooded Cherokee. Even though my cousin Marygail researched our family tree extensively and was not able to readily identify her, we all remain convinced and very proud, I might add, of our Native American lineage. The proof-positive for me is found in my grandfather's dark skin, my mother's beautiful high cheekbones, and her severe lactose intolerance. My mother loved ice cream but would typically react within minutes of consuming it; more often than not, she and I were together when she enjoyed the frozen treat, and we would have to find a bathroom quickly. Sometimes we would be traveling or playing golf and the best we could do was the "green latrine." (Author's note: It is estimated that between 80-100% of North American indigenous people are lactose intolerant.)

My mother was also a make-up minimalist, her natural beauty allowing her to get away with it. When she was a child, she very much enjoyed lying across a bed watching her favorite aunt, Lillian (my grandmother's youngest sibling), apply her makeup in advance of a date; but apparently she just enjoyed the closeness and the mindless joy of watching a practiced routine and didn't pattern the ritual. To my knowledge, the only makeup Mom ever wore was face powder, a little rouge, and lipstick—her color of choice always evident on a scrap of paper bearing her lip-prints in her purse.

My parents' social life was also intertwined with the church. The adults, especially the ones with small children like me, would frequently gather for various events: cookouts, board games, broadcasted college football games, and Rook—a card game that I learned by sitting in one parent's lap or the other and watching the interplay of the four participants. I can remember sitting in Dad's lap and hearing him whisper teaching tips into my ear, explaining briefly why he had played this card or that.

Interacting with these other church families, sometimes in their homes, I learned the art and science of good behavior. My parents were in lock-step in their belief that a child should be seen and not heard and were both absolutely committed to Proverbs 13:24, paraphrased—spare the rod and spoil the child. They were certainly aligned philosophically on this subject; however, their implementation differed, sometimes radically. Mom's lines between acceptable and unacceptable behavior were crystal clear, and I knew exactly where they were and understood them. Basically, doing something I was told explicitly not to do, talking back to her or sassing, or being disrespectful to anyone or their property would guarantee me a spanking. Mom would almost always use one of Daddy's belts, but would never threaten me with him. She took care of business herself and believed that threatening a child with later punishment when "your father gets home" would only make the child dread their father's arrival and could potentially sabotage the father-child relationship. She would strike me only on the buttocks or my legs, never in the face—she thought slapping someone in the face was demeaning; she believed it went way beyond simply administering punishment for bad behavior and crossed over into humiliation and disrespect. She also administered my discipline in private, again, in an attempt to avoid humiliation and disrespect. The stated goal of her disciplinary philosophy was to "break my will, but never crush my spirit."

My father's lines between acceptable and unacceptable behavior, on the other hand, moved around in mercurial fashion. For sure, the big three—disobedience, back-talking, and disrespect—would trigger him; but other things would push his buttons as well, and I didn't fully understand them. The time and the place didn't matter much to him either. With my father, retribution was swift.

Years later, when I was in my twenties, my father offered me an apology, out of the blue as I remember it, saying he hoped I would forgive him because when I was a child sometimes he would discipline me trying to set an example for the parents of the other children who were behaving in some manner that he found unacceptable. I took this confession in stride and told him not to worry himself as I was certainly no worse for wear. He was so contrite that I could only, in good conscience, offer him the mercy that he obviously wished he had afforded me.

Mom had her own guilt regarding this part of Dad's disciplinary tactics. She also shared, decades later, that she cringed whenever Daddy would administer a "substitution spanking"; her intervention was held at bay by her belief that parents should present a united front to their children. She did add one caveat, however. She told me, with a wink and a wry smile, that if he had ever gone one inch past ordinary spanking into the realm of child abuse she would have shot him. I believed her.

My mother used to say, "Honey, you didn't come with a rule book tied around your neck; your Dad and I did the best we could." I honestly believe that both my parents did the best they could; and I knew beyond the shadow of a doubt that I was loved beyond measure and that I could trust them. On the early training ground that was Birmingham, Alabama, I learned the importance of treating all living creatures with dignity and respect; I learned what good behavior looked like; I learned that I was not the center of the universe; I learned that money did not grow on trees; and I learned that Jesus loved me. Not a bad start for the first seven years of one's life.

2

In the late 1960s, exciting work opportunities at the Kennedy Space Center, near Titusville, Florida, began to open up. Spurred forward by President Kennedy's challenge to go to the moon, NASA and the companies with which they subcontracted were looking, in earnest, for scientists, engineers, administrators, and skilled craftsmen of every ilk. My father was a first rate mechanic—a John Steinbeck *Cannery Row* kind of mechanic, no formal training but able to diagnose an engine's ailment with his ears and able to make it literally purr with a simple tweak. Thankfully, Dad didn't share the *Cannery Row* mechanic's predilection for alcohol. His addictions were coffee and cigarettes, the latter being the central element of his rather early death at age seventy-five. In 1967, Dad applied for a mechanic's position with the Bendix Corporation, an engineering company that provided operational support for the Apollo program, and to my parents' delight, was awarded a job. Excited by the prospects of this new adventure, my parents and I packed up and moved to Florida shortly after I completed the first grade.

Everything about the move to Florida was an upgrade. We bought a concrete block house in a nice neighborhood, walking distance from the Indian River; the U.S. Highway 1 side of said river was the prime viewing location for the launch of the Apollo moon missions. During the seven and one-half years that we lived in Titusville, we witnessed eleven launches of the powerful Saturn V rocket, including Apollo 11, the first manned landing on the moon in 1969. In the re-telling of the launch experience, my mom, fascinated with the effects the rockets would have as they broke the sound barrier, would say, "Your britches legs would actually shake." My father loved his work and would bring home interesting souvenirs for me and beautiful large, framed, glossy photographs of the moon and Earth from space. All three of us found this era of space exploration fascinating and were thrilled to be so close to it.

Our proximity to Orlando and Walt Disney World was a definite plus, and my parents often opened our home to visiting friends and family from Alabama. Only once do I remember a family of friends coming very close to overstaying their welcome—when the third full week of their vacation came and went and they were still staying at our house. I recall overhearing my parents quietly discussing the various options available to them to kindly send the message that these folks were eating us out of house and home. My parents decided that Mom would invite the matriarch of the brood to go grocery shopping with her in hopes this would spark some sort of recognition that they needed to contribute. To my recollection, she did offer to help with the groceries and my mother eagerly accepted. Lesson learned for me, "Don't ride a free horse to death."

Our new neighborhood had two floor plans that repeated in every-other fashion up and down the blocks, all of which featured nice wide sidewalks. The new Florida house was quite different from the Alabama house. Our new home had a two-car garage instead of an open air carport, three bedrooms instead of two, two bathrooms instead of one, and central air and heat. Instead of the Alabama brick, there was the Florida concrete block; instead of the Alabama wood floors, there were the cold and unforgiving but interesting terrazzo floors.

Except for the occasional strong thunderstorm or hurricane that brewed in the Caribbean and then traveled up the east coast of Florida, the weather was very nice; and the warmer winters brought immediate relief from the ear aches and respiratory infections I had struggled with in Birmingham. By far the best upgrade, however, was the fact that my father's salary got enough of a bump to facilitate my mom no longer having to work. So, from second grade on she was available for me, and in retrospect her availability played a huge role in the positive relationship we were able to build and maintain.

Not wanting to burn any bridges in case this new opportunity didn't pan out, my dad and I traveled to Florida first and allowed Mom to stay behind to work out a two-week notice with the telephone company, thereby departing on good terms. I remember Dad and me touring the brand new house he had purchased for us, and except for the gigantic flies audibly knocking against the windows to get out, I thought it was grand. We had a list of things to accomplish before Mom arrived, and one of our top priorities was getting me enrolled in school. Part of that process was a physical, of sorts, that basically checked the child's hearing and vision and ensured all the appropriate vaccinations were up to date. During the eye exam, my father questioned the county nurse by saying, "She didn't do very well on that, did she?" The nurse, I reasoned in later years, was overwhelmed by the demands of her position and answered my father rather flippantly, "Oh, she did fine." So, with that behind me, I was enrolled in second grade at Coquina Elementary School, in Titusville, Florida.

Upon arriving for the first day of school, I marveled at the very large orange-pink rock that lay just beneath the school sign. I had seen nothing like it in my experience to date and, upon closer inspection, realized it was made of millions of tiny shells. I knew this was the kind of detail my mother would find interesting, and later we researched it together and learned the geological name of the rock was coquina—thus the name of my school. My Florida school was designed differently than my Alabama school. In Alabama, the first grade classroom was a large open room with an entire wall of windows, covering three-quarters of the height of the walls and looking outside onto the covered sidewalk that led to the main hallway of the school. Coquina Elementary was set up in pods connected by sidewalks. Basically each grade level was contained within a pod, and within each pod there were several classrooms. Homeroom and reading were in one classroom, while math and science were in a different classroom a short walk away. History and spelling were actually taught in a trailer near the playground at the back of the second-grade pod.

I specifically remember my third-grade math teacher. She would use her blackboard extensively to illustrate this or that about numbers. Although I could see my paper and my handwritten numbers clearly, I found it very difficult to see the blackboard from my seat on the back row. I had somehow learned through experimentation that if I pulled my eyelids into slits I could see the board significantly better and thought nothing of this workaround. Having no basis for comparison, I thought my poor distance vision was completely natural. One day, she called on me to read something from the board; so I assumed my long distance viewing position, resting my chin in the V formed by the heels of my hands touching, and then using my middle fingers to pull the skin at the outside corner of my eyes back toward my temples. When I did this, the numbers came into focus and I gave my teacher the information she had asked for. After class that very day, she asked me to give a handwritten note she had scribed to my mother. She assured me I was not in any kind of trouble but emphasized that it was very important that Mom or Dad get the note. So I dutifully delivered it to my parents.

The substance of the note turned out to be advice for my parents to seek an appointment for me with her husband, a local optometrist. I vividly recall sitting in the optometrist's chair and staring straight ahead at the lighted rectangle at the end of the examining room. Mom was sitting to my right in a visitor's chair. When the doctor asked me to read the top line (the big E), I told him I couldn't see anything on the lighted white background. I recall, off to my right side, hearing my mother exhale a long, soft "ohhhhhh" that diminished in tone and volume over a few seconds until it was only breath. It did not contain words, but spoke volumes—she said without saying, "I have let my baby down."

As it turned out, I needed glasses badly. My first pair was actually bifocals, and I remember donning them for the first time and seeing my first tree. Years later my mother shared with me an emotion she had dealt with upon our first visit to the optometrist. She confessed that she had prayed while I was still in the womb that I would be born with beautiful eyes. She said it had been her experience that people with beautiful eyes just seemed to have an easier time garnering other people's respect; she wanted that for me. Her exhale that day at the doctor's office was actually a realization of sorts as she concluded, then and there, a better prayer would have been to ask that I be born with healthy eyes.

A judgment of beauty is certainly in the eyes of the beholder, but over the years I have been told from time to time that my eyes were beautiful. In fact, I have been told I have "talking eyes." My mom made me laugh with the story of my maternal grandmother holding me for the first time just months after I was born and telling my mother, "If this baby speaks to me, I am going to throw her down and run."

During our Florida years, the child-rearing work my parents had begun in Birmingham continued as their commitment to my development stayed foremost in their priorities. Many times through their example, but also by their commitment to our church, they helped me along the path to adulthood by giving me the opportunity to develop strong core values. Attributes such as compassion, generosity, understanding, and forgiveness were modeled by my mother and other influential adults in my parents' lives. My father was great testimony to the value of responsibility and hard work and taking care of one's family. Over time, naturally, both of my parents teetered atop the unrealistic pedestal I had erected for them. Their imperfections should have served as validation for me that everyone, no matter who they are, will fall short of their goals from time to time; but I was becoming a perfectionist and in my young mind there was simply no room for failure. I certainly could not see perfectionism as a future potential problem, but it would become one. Then, just as she had done dozens of times before, my sweet mother would come to the rescue with a wise anecdote that in its simplicity would ring authentic and clear.

Although my father's work at the Cape was a full-time job, including occasional opportunities to work overtime, he also engaged in mechanical work in our garage for the simple enjoyment of it. He could do almost anything with a level of skill that made him valuable to his friends when they engaged in their own do-it-yourself projects around their homes. I was the benefactor of several of his projects, as go-carts, mini-bikes, and dune buggies were fixtures of my adolescent years. My favorite bequeathment was the old green English Ford my father bought for a pittance and allowed me to drive up and down our fifty-foot-long driveway after he got it running again. My best friend Joyce and I would take turns driving, with the other one of us sitting in the front passenger seat—reverse then forward, reverse then forward. We probably logged a thousand miles in fifty-foot increments on that old car.

Since my father stayed busy with work of some fashion and seemed to be happy doing so, the majority of my down time from school during those years was spent with my mother. I remember my relationship with my mother during that time being one of significant companionship. She never stepped back from being the mother, nor did she shy away from the being the disciplinarian, but we played together a lot during our Florida years; the first seeds of genuine friendship were sown there, and when I became an adult, the friendship blossomed.

My mother was a superb athlete and enjoyed playing a myriad of sports. During her high school years she played tennis and softball and even lettered in basketball her junior and senior years. My grandfather's work with the Tennessee Valley Authority was transitional, and therefore the family moved around a great deal during Mom's high school years. Aunt Millie, the second born, recalled it being much easier to be initially accepted by the students in the new schools as the younger sister of the impressively athletic Kathryn Adams.

My grandfather passed away from leukopenia at the age of forty-seven; so all of my knowledge of him comes to me through stories told by his wife and children. My mother recounted a story that told me a great deal about his fatherly instincts, and I find pride in the telling as did my mother. During one of her high school basketball games with my grandfather in attendance, she apparently lost her infamous temper and got ejected from the game. Everything was going along fine until the referee placed his hand on her shoulder. Mom recalled my grandfather appearing to have been supernaturally transported from his seat in the bleachers to the gymnasium floor where she stood. He told the referee in a calm yet stern voice, "You were right to eject her, but don't you ever lay your hands on her again."

During her nurse's training days in Atlanta, she actually pitched for a semi-professional fast pitch softball team. I delighted in hearing her stories about playing with the fast pitch team, and ever the teacher, my mom once again illustrated an excellent lesson when she told the story of her first start on the mound for the Blue-Sox. She recalled being in the zone, throwing strike after strike. Between innings, as she returned to the dugout, she recalled her coach saying, "Ease up Kathy; you are going to get tired; let your fielders help you out." Advice she apparently ignored because about five innings into the game, her pitches became slower and predictable, and the other team began to lace them at will. Mom lost that game but used the story as a teaching point for me—listening to the advice of more experienced people is rarely a bad thing.

My mother was also a good golfer and put a club in my hands when I was about twelve years old. I don't know the history of her interest in the sport but somewhere along the way her natural athleticism led her to it. She became a student of the game and taught me so much about its demand for balance and gracefulness and its perpetual offers of redemption. She taught me to grip the club only tight enough to keep it from flying out of my hands. "Pretend," she would say, "that the club is an open tube of toothpaste and during the swing try not to push any paste out—let the club do the work." She taught me that even after a bad shot you have an immediate opportunity to make a brilliant shot and that keeping your head still and down through the swing can cover a multitude of "golf sins." I find, as she did, that the rules of golf closely resemble the rules of a good life.

It was not surprising to me that she took such an interest in this complicated and mentally demanding sport because that was a quality of her personality—she took an interest in things. I have vivid memories of her telling me, before it became state of the art, to watch for the laser beam to eventually change the way we all live—prophetic. She told me once of a memory she had of her physics professor in high school, holding up a piece of chalk, and saying, "If we ever figure out what is holding this piece of chalk together, it will be one of man's most significant discoveries." As a ten-year-old, I remember her coming into my room around midnight one night and suggesting that I bring my newly acquired telescope into hers and Daddy's bedroom (he was working overtime) and train it on the moon, which was completely visible and framed by their front bedroom window. I remember being thrilled and surprised that my mother would suggest such a thing so late at night. It was a beautiful moon, full and bright and huge, and we had fun comparing what we were viewing through the lens with the giant illustrated poster of the moon that I had retrieved from the back of my bedroom door and laid out across my parents' bed. We traded intakes of breath and the phrase "Okay, let me see" back and forth for hours.

When I was about eight years old, I benefited from another thrilling surprise handcrafted by my mother—a passenger train trip for the two of us from Titusville to Pensacola, home of Aunt Millie and her family. As I reflect back on that experience today, I chalk the idea up to my mother's propensity to wonder and explore. Whether through her intuition or through something she read that predicted passenger train travel would soon be a thing of the past, she decided she wanted me to experience it before the industry was mothballed. We had a wonderful time. We boarded early in the morning and actually ordered and ate breakfast in the dining car. A handsome black waiter in white tailcoat served us French toast under a silver dome and hot chocolate from a silver tea service. Needless to say, I had never before experienced such finery.

In the middle of my fifth-grade year, my parents decided we would take a family vacation and go south, down into the wide body of Florida. I reasoned the odd timing to be associated with the fact there would be fewer people vacationing during the school year. My mother requested permission from my fifth-grade teacher; my teacher obtained the appropriate permissions from the principal; and everyone agreed to the two-week hiatus provided I complete all of my requisite homework assignments for the next two weeks and hand those in upon my return. My mother declared that I would work on those assignments each evening in the hotel room just as if I were home, which is exactly what I did.

I remember a visit to the Ringling Bros. and Barnum & Bailey Circus museum near Sarasota and being called up on stage, as the only child in the audience, to participate in the puppet show. The best stop however was our time at the winter retreat of Thomas Edison in Fort Myers. My mother eagerly soaked up every Edison detail she heard or read, remembering events of his early life for the later re-telling, such as being pulled onto a moving train by his ears as a youngster, which eventually rendered him deaf. When the tour guide told us the light bulb sitting on the mantle in the Edison home had been burning for dozens of years, Mom commented under her breath, "Well, they surely don't make them like they used to."

The huge banyan trees growing on the grounds of his home were also fascinating; and Mom memorized the specifics of the tree's unique ability to make future minor trunks in the early form of spindly roots growing down from its many branches, eventually creating a maze of strong tree legs around each main trunk. This vacation was the most fun time I recall ever having with both my parents together.

Aside from raising me, there was one other thing that completely bonded my parents—Alabama Crimson Tide football. My parents and later I, by example, would get so nervous before and during a game, one might think we had our life savings on the line. That was never the case, but we were just short of fanatical. My memories of either watching or listening to Alabama football games with my parents are numerous and vivid. One such memory features my father, standing in the kitchen of our Florida home, listening to a small white plastic radio as it broadcast the 1967 contest between the Tide and the LSU Tigers. I can still see him—standing adjacent to and leaning sideways against the kitchen counter, one bare foot slightly in front of the other, in shorts and T-shirt, bent over at the waist, right elbow on the counter, a cigarette pointing skyward clamped between the first two fingers of his right hand while his head is resting in his palm. He is staring down at the floor, transfixed and tense, waiting to hear if, after three scoreless quarters, the lone touchdown Alabama has scored in the fourth quarter will hold. He groans when LSU scores a touchdown of their own later in the fourth quarter and resumes the thousand yard stare as the Bengal Tigers line up for the point-after attempt. The smoke from his cigarette is thin, ribbony, and gently curling upward—until the place kicker misses the PAT that would have tied the game. Then the ribbon of smoke, no longer thin and gently curling, traces every move of his wild victory dance.

In 1971, Alabama had reeled off eleven straight wins and was slated to face the Nebraska Cornhuskers in the Orange Bowl in Miami, Florida, on January 1, 1972, ostensibly for the national championship. The college football bowl games typically occurred around the Christmas and New Year's holiday; so we were either in Birmingham with our family or in Dadeville, Alabama, with Ms. Nita and Mr. Eugene.

But wherever we were, the television was tuned to the game. The Cornhuskers blew the Tide out of the water in a 38-6 lopsided victory. Our drive back to Titusville the next day was made even longer as we collectively mourned the loss. When we finally pulled into the driveway of our house, it was after dark and the headlights of our car panned across our closed garage door as we made the turn. My father stopped the car short, and both my parents leaned forward in the front seat trying to make out the words on some sort of lettered sign taped askew to the metal skin of the garage door. In the light provided by our low beams, Mom was finally able to make it out and read aloud,—"What's that I smell? Must be a low tide." Dad giggled resignedly and Mom said, "That has to be that stinking Bob."

She was talking about our next door neighbor, who was a California native and pulled for all teams California. He delighted in giving my parents fits about the performance or lack thereof of the Crimson Tide.

The only participative sport I recall my parents engaging in together was bowling. They were in a mixed league and bowled on the same team one night a week while we lived in Birmingham, and most of the time I was in attendance. My father threw a beautiful curve ball that made a fascinating trek down the alley; although right-handed, he would approach from the left, and lay the ball down, spinning hard counter-clockwise in that same left corner, but would throw it toward the right gutter. As it approached the right gutter about three-quarters of the way down the alley, it would make a dramatic left hand turn just in time to contact the head pin and its neighbor on the right. He usually obtained wonderful pin action, and I loved to watch him bowl. My mother threw a fast twelve-pound ball from the right side with a simple back spin that found the mark on the "Brooklyn side" of the strike zone, as she liked to call it. As soon as I was strong enough to lift a ball, Mom taught me how to bowl, and I enjoyed being a part of a Saturday morning bowling league for children for a number of years while we lived in Titusville.

My enjoyment came from more than just watching my parents bowl however; it seemed to be a time when they were teammates certainly, but also actually friends. When my mother would throw a strike or pick up a nice spare, my father would use the affectionate language with her that brought me such joy, such as "Nice ball, Kat" or "Good shot, Momma." He automatically corrected himself when he called her by her name in front of me because of my tendency as a very young child to call them by their first names instead of Momma and Daddy.

The other occasion when Dad would sometimes use the affectionate language with my mother was when we were on a long road trip as a family. Living in Florida now, we were an eight-hour drive from Birmingham and most of the rest of our family. We typically made the trip over Thanksgiving and Christmas and generally made it in one day. My parents would take turns driving; and when it was Mom's turn to drive, Daddy would get into the back seat and take a nap (he could sleep anywhere, a gift that he bestowed on me). He would wait, however, until Mom was on the right road and headed in the right direction before he allowed himself to nod off. When she reached the cruising speed, he would say, "Momma's found a bug; now she's gonna' let her eat," and with that he would stretch out and get comfortable—"her" in this case was our 1967 maroon two-door Chevrolet Impala SS with the white vinyl landau top. I would sit in the front seat with Mom, who was an excellent driver, and watch contentedly out the window, listening to the Platters on the eight-track cassette player and Dad snoring softly from the back seat.

I attended Coquina Elementary for only two years. Shortly after I finished the third grade, construction was completed on a brand new school located on the back side of our subdivision. Imperial Estates Elementary School took its name from the subdivision we lived in, and I completed grades four through six there. It employed a clever arrangement of classrooms, libraries, and work spaces for the teachers and students. There was a center concrete courtyard surrounded by six complexes. Complex A had a large red double door with a huge black "A" painted on it and was the first grade classroom. Complex B, the second grade classroom, was a yellow door with a huge black "B." These two complexes shared a library in the middle, with each complex having a set of restrooms, a large lecture room with an elevated stage at one end, a smaller glassed-in classroom, and a medium sized classroom that could be walled off by accordion doors. The teachers for each grade shared office space, which like the library was situated between the two complexes. This same arrangement was used for

Complexes C and D, third and fourth grades, and Complexes E and F, fifth and sixth grades. All of these complexes were covered by a gigantic elevated roof that provided enough overhang to protect the complexes and the inside courtyard from rain but allowed air and light to come in around its entire perimeter. In the very center of the courtyard was an approximate fifteen-foot by fifteen-foot sunken concrete square, featuring a covered drain at its low point and two flights of concrete steps around all four sides. We often ate lunch sitting on those steps, balancing our sandwiches on our thighs and setting our drinks down beside us on the concrete. The walkway just outside each complex's door also featured a painted hopscotch grid, where we would occupy our time in friendly competition as we waited for classes to start.

The best thing about the new school, however, was its proximity to our homes. My friends and I could ride our bikes to school and never have to leave the confines of the neighborhood. My mother and Joyce's mother were circumspect about the new teaching techniques brought on by the unique design of the complexes, but loved the fact that the new school was so close to home.

Virtually every day I would have homework, and the rules were that homework had to be done before television or outside activities. I was a good student, enjoyed learning, and rarely was tempted to procrastinate with my studies (I saved all of my procrastination for my chores, especially dish-washing), but my mother would never let me dive immediately into my assignments. She thought it was important to take a mental break between the end of the school day and the beginning of homework. She would usually give me a glass of milk, maybe some cookies, and would ask about my day. Sometimes we would role play; I would be the dusty cowboy coming in off the trail and ask for a whiskey. Mom would take down the shot glass we owned (odd, because the only alcoholic beverage in our house was vanilla flavoring) and fill it with Coca-Cola. Sometimes I would shoot it and ask the "bartender" for another. We had seen enough episodes of "Bonanza" and "Gunsmoke" to keep up the dialogue until one us got tickled.

Directly behind our house, about fifty yards from our backyard fence, was an unpaved trail large enough for a car to travel on, and adjacent to the trail were dozens of acres of public woods in which my friends and I loved to play. We could spend hours at a time exploring the woods— building forts and climbing trees—periodically and dutifully reappearing at our back fence and waving to my mother signaling we were all okay. The acreage was full of smaller bike-sized trails that ran willy-nilly through the pine and scrub oak woods; the car-sized trail wound around the edge of the woods and up a sizable hill, by Florida standards, to a community water tower. Just beyond the water tower was my mother's playground. Sand dunes abounded behind the tower, and my mother fearlessly drove the dune buggy that my father had built around and over the dunes, absolutely delighting when she was able to top a dune and launch the buggy off the crest, making all four tires leave the ground simultaneously. She even set me up with a camera one day in a strategic location and had me capture her stunt on film. She was far braver than I, the dune buggy bringing out the daredevil in her.

Our new double garage was my father's playground, and during our years in Florida he actually constructed two dune buggies. I recall him discussing the "formula" for building a buggy. First, he had to locate an old, inexpensive VW Beetle. He would then scrap the body, remove seventeen and one-half inches from the length of the frame, making the cut right behind the front seats, and then weld the two halves back together. Concurrent with the frame preparation, he would begin the search for a fiberglass body. Our first buggy was a red metal flake that was actually someone's experiment as they tried to blend a silver metal flake border around the edge of the body. It didn't blend very well and consequently didn't look so good, which made it quite inexpensive. Ever the bargain hunter, my dad jumped on the deal. Next, he would shop for front seats, used wide tires, and the mandatory roll bar. The transmission on this first buggy was what Dad termed as "not synchronized," meaning the buggy had to be at a near complete stop before it could be shifted into first gear. This feature was certainly a limitation for a buggy; so, basking in the success of his first foray into dune buggy building, he soon began working on another, selling the first to help finance the second. The second buggy was a brown metal flake with a newer model VW engine and synchronized transmission. It was lighter and more versatile and capable of keeping up with the thrill seeker side of my mother's personality.

As a family, we enjoyed the dune buggies very much. Sometimes we would ride the woods with another family who owned a dune buggy. I remember a post-ride photo of Mom and some friends of my parents following a full afternoon of trailing my Dad and me in our buggy along miles of dusty Florida trails. When the ride was over the only bright parts of Mom and the other couple were their teeth and the whites of their eyes. They were filthy and Mom delighted in capturing the adventure for all time to come in a photo. The sheer joy on her face in that photo is a permanent fixture in my memory. If I were a painter, I could replicate its every detail without ever physically seeing it again.

My mother was a huge fan of capturing her life and later our life on film. I still have dozens of photos of her in her younger years, involved in various activities with sports teams, boyfriends, girlfriends, and family. When I was a very young child, she purchased a hand-held movie camera and captured a rare snowfall in Birmingham with me, looking like a tiny Eskimo, standing in it. For indoor pre-arranged activities such as my first birthday, she purchased a bar light in order to provide enough illumination for the filming. I still have that movie, which records the members of my Birmingham family coming to our house to celebrate with us. Mom was careful to catch each and every attendee by calling out to them and having them show their faces to the camera. The film had no sound, but their quick head turns and squinting eyes were sure signs that the bar light had momentarily blinded them as they responded to my mother's request to look her way.

As photographic and video-graphic technology became more sophisticated over the years, Mom tried to keep up. I remember her purchasing an 8-mm movie projector that looked very much like the reel-to-reel projectors one might see in a movie theatre, albeit a much smaller version; she also bought a slide projector. She was an organized person by nature, and the carousels full of slides were carefully catalogued and the reels of movies were thoughtfully labeled. One of my most treasured memories of spending one-on-one time with my mother involved me introducing her to 1990s camcorder technology.

It was 1996, and she and I had joined Aunt Millie and a family friend on a trip to Fontana, North Carolina, for a high school class reunion. My mother and my aunt had attended the high school in Fontana for two years in the mid 1940s, before their father was transferred to Georgia. The participants in the reunion (which, at this writing, will soon commence for the thirtieth straight year) called themselves "The Dam Kids," because of their affiliation with Fontana Dam, a vital TVA project that broke ground, with U. S. government support, just weeks after the attack on Pearl Harbor and employed thousands of men, including my grandfather.

The four of us had rented a cabin in the mountains; and while my mother and aunt certainly looked forward to the reunion, we all looked forward to a few days of beautiful scenery and the peacefulness of the Great Smoky Mountains. Shortly after we arrived at the cabin and had settled in, Mom and I decided to drive to Cade's Cove, a lush, picturesque valley located in the Tennessee section of the Smokies about two hours away. When we arrived, I pulled over to the side of the road, got out the camcorder, and gave Mom a quick tutorial on its operation. Unbeknownst to both of us, while she tried to familiarize herself with the controls and figure out the meaning of the small icons on the screen, the camcorder was recording.

It captured a hilarious conversation between us, as Mom, while looking through the viewfinder and turning the recorder this way and that, asked comical questions such as, "What am I looking at?" "Is this thing on?" "What cows?" It also recorded unintelligible instructions from me that could not be deciphered because of my debilitating laughter. We decided to continue our drive around the Cove; so I intentionally checked to make sure the camera was off and handed it back to her. Very soon we came upon a beautiful horse standing near a fence alongside the road and I suggested that Mom should film him. By this time, she was trying to learn the art of zooming in. She said, camcorder in hand pointed toward the animal, "He's looking at me mean," and "Oh dear, all I can see is his nose." We both dissolved into laughter at this comment and for several seconds the audio on the tape appears to go away, but it is actually us laughing so hard we are unable to make any sound. The final VHS tape we made that day, partly planned and partly accidental, is a treasured possession of mine and shows shots of the inside of the car, her feet, the sky, tiny distant cows, the tops of trees, a horse's eye, and a hairy nose. Every time I view it, I become physically weak with laughter.

Another remarkable thing took place on that particular trip. As we were driving from the Cove back to the cabin, Mom wondered out loud if her handsome old boyfriend B. still lived in the area. She pointed out a dirt road and said she thought she remembered that he had lived on it. So, more than anything else, to humor her and to extend our lovely day together, I turned onto the road. To my total astonishment, just moments later we rounded a curve and spotted a mailbox with his last name printed on it. In the driveway of that house we could see an older man and a younger man with their heads close together and bent over under the hood of a parked car.

I stopped on the side of the road, and Mom and I discussed the merits of me approaching him and asking him if he indeed was her old boyfriend. Curiosity killed the cat; so I got out of the car, set the brake, left it running, and walked up the driveway. I introduced myself and asked if he remembered a young lady by the name of Kathryn Adams. He cocked his head a little to one side and furrowed his brow searching his memory for her name and face. Seconds later he said yes, of course he remembered Kathryn Adams. I told him well, she remembers you also, happens to be my mother, and is sitting in the car parked at the bottom of your driveway. He introduced his grandson, the young man we had seen from the street, and then followed me. Mom had rolled her window down and B. walked to her side of the car, bent down a little, folded his arms on the sill, and looked in at her. They exchanged small talk for a few seconds and then he said, "You are still a good-looking woman." I quickly turned my head away, as if to give them privacy, and rolled my eyes a little. In the tiny movie that was being played out in front of me, I could easily envision a scene, fifty years earlier, featuring the lovely, coy young lady enjoying the attention from the dashing young man; I couldn't help but smile.

As a family, Mom, Dad, and I made several trips to the Smokies over the years. Sometimes we went with friends, and sometimes with family. But, by far, my most memorable trip to those beautiful mountains is the one where Mom and I bent double with laughter in Cade's Cove and remained astonished for years that we had happened upon her old flame, B.

My parent's affiliation with the church continued in Florida, and after a couple of visits we soon joined the congregation at a medium-sized church in downtown Titusville. My Dad joined the choir and served as a deacon; and Mom taught Sunday School, participated in the Women's Missionary Union (WMU), and helped with the youth. I remember this congregation being full of really fine people, as best as someone my age could judge that.

Every fifth Sunday we had "dinner on the ground," replete with food either baked and brought from the kitchens of the members or picked up from a local restaurant on the way to services earlier that morning. Mom would usually bring either English pea casserole, which was good, or her home-made potato salad, which was heavenly, a characteristic she credited to the fact that she boiled the potatoes in their "jackets."

Our eating area was a large grassy spot in a copse of pines at the back of the church property that was home to several stationary concrete tables, about four feet wide, set up end to end, and running for about forty feet. The ladies of the church would dress the concrete tables in vinyl red-checkered table cloths and then place dozens of plates, platters, and bowls full of food on top. Our pastor offered thanks for the bounty prior to dismissing the congregation from the Sunday morning service. So as soon as the food was out, we would line up at one end of the tables and begin serving our plates: selecting, reaching, dipping, moving slowly en masse down the length of red-checkered vinyl from stacks of paper and plastic ware to the meats, the vegetables, the relishes, the breads, and finally, the desserts. I would always save enough room on my plate for a scoop of whatever Momma had brought because I knew how good it would be.

Small knots of people, carefully balancing paper plates full of food, either in one hand or atop their tightly closed knees, dotted the sunshine dappled grassy spot, and conversation mixed with laughter abounded. Those wonderful Sundays usually began to break up around three in the afternoon; but not before the youth managed to squeeze in a game of touch football, where around the age of ten I began to showcase the tight spiral my mother had taught me to throw.

Youth activities were very important to that church, and I remember my mother being involved with those programs in a significant way. In contrast to her otherwise stoic nature, finding fun and entertaining activities to accompany the Bible lessons was something she did very well. I specifically remember two games she introduced to the youth and the other teachers. One was in truth a brain teaser, and it was fun to watch the people who thought they had figured out the "trick" come to the realization that they had not.

The game started with Mom placing nine books on the floor in a three-by-three grid. Next, one person (who understood how the game worked) would leave the room while a second person would choose one of the nine books and then tell my mother which book they had chosen. When the first person returned, Mom would systematically point to the books on the floor with a yardstick, and ask, "Is this the one?" Without fail, the person who had been sequestered would guess which book had been chosen. The others would shout randomly, "I got it! It's the third book you point to"; or "It's the fifth book you point to right after you say the words, 'Are you sure?' " To further demonstrate their "special powers of concentration" the person in the know would again leave the room, and Mom would make sure she didn't reveal the chosen book using any of the previous guesswork; and again, the sequestered person would choose the right book, and everyone else would be baffled. Occasionally, someone would indeed figure out the code, ask to leave the room, and then return triumphant, choosing the correct book.

The trick was in the pointing. Whichever book was chosen in the three by three grid, Mom would place the yardstick on the face of the first book she pointed to in the exact spot of the corresponding grid location of the chosen book. For example, if the middle book was chosen, on her first point regardless of the book she pointed to, she would place the yardstick in the exact center of the book face. That would signal the guesser that the chosen book had been the one in the middle.

The other game that delighted the youth, and soon became an initiation of sorts for any newcomers, was the egg game. Mom would bring a dozen fresh eggs and lay them on the floor in a wide pattern. She would then get the newcomer to participate by asking them to take a few moments to memorize the pattern of the eggs and then walk blindfolded from one end of the egg pattern to the other. The trick was that while the newcomer was distracted with instructions and the act of being blindfolded, we helpers would quickly pick up all the eggs. Mom would assure the blindfolded young person that they would be getting helpful encouragement from the rest of us. It was very funny watching this blindfolded person take extremely careful steps and respond to any and all warnings from the onlookers by adjusting their next step in the nick of time, sometimes having to suspend on one leg, trying to remember a safe place whereon to put that foot, and responding to yells of "Yeah, yeah, that's a good spot!" In the end, when the blindfolded participant had made it "safely" across the room, the blindfold was removed and they were allowed to look back at the empty floor they had just painstakingly crossed. It was always good for a hearty laugh by onlookers and victim.

By far her funniest prank was the one known as Kissing the Royal Ring. She did this only once and chose one of her favorites, a teenager whom I will call Sally, to be blindfolded and brought before royalty to kiss the ring. Mom had borrowed one of the senior youth's class ring and put it on the hand of another youth dressed in pretend robe and crown. Sally was led in blindfolded and told to kiss the ring, which she reluctantly did. All this time, Mom is telling the story of how shy the king is and how he cannot stand to be looked at. After Sally had bent down and kissed the ring on the hand of the other youth, we quickly took the ring off his finger, put it on his bare toe, and had him raise his foot close to the same level. Then Mom removed Sally's blindfold. When she saw the ring on his toe, she assumed that was what she had kissed, and her gag reflex went into overdrive. We all laughed hilariously, and much to her relief we quickly revealed to her that she had not really kissed his nasty toes.

Although I was a pre-teen during my mother's work with the teenaged youth of the church, I was included many times at their gatherings and began to see, for the first time, how my mother was viewed through the eyes of other people. It was not lost on me that some of the older teenagers and even some young adults sought her out for advice and counsel.

Sally, the Royal Ring victim, was certainly one of Mom's admirers. She was the eldest of four and lived with her parents, a younger brother, and two younger sisters. Her father was a devout Christian, even giving up his job as a store manager when the store began to sell alcohol.

Unfortunately, his beliefs also included a strong conviction that females should remain in submissive roles and therefore had made no plans nor provisions for Sally or either of her sisters to go to college. He had begun to save money to send his son to college but not the girls. Sally found her father's ways archaic and hurtful. I was not privy to the counseling my mother gave Sally, but the obvious affection and respect that she had for my mother signaled to me that it had helped her.

I also have memories of another young woman whom Mom counseled, whom I will call Patricia. Patricia was new to our church and in her early twenties when she and my mother met. She was, at the time, dating a very handsome young man for whom she professed to have deep feelings. He wanted to marry her, but she was reluctant because he did not share her need for a church-centered life and had a fondness for alcohol. I happened to be in the back seat of our car one Sunday evening after services as Mom and Patricia talked. Mom counseled that it was unrealistic to expect that he would change after they were married. She did not advise against the marriage but simply told Patricia to go in with her eyes wide open and not to marry him thinking that she could change him. I honestly don't know what decision she finally made, as a job transfer made a move away from Titusville necessary for her. I do know, however, how grateful she appeared to be to have someone like my mother with whom to talk.

One summer, I remember Mom taking on the responsibility of teaching the pre-teens in Vacation Bible School. This two-week Bible-based training occurred annually at every church I had ever been affiliated with, and I tried to look forward to it. But after a long school year, the last thing I wanted to do was attend two more weeks of "school," even if it was less structured and more fun. This particular summer, my mother, following a professionally assembled outline for the two weeks of biblically based instruction, taught the section on rights—individual rights. I remember this illustration as if it were yesterday. She called on me to step to the center of the room. This surprised me a little because she was very careful to avoid any appearances of favoritism. She asked me to stand in one place and swing my arms back and forth by my sides, and to keep it up. Then she asked one of the boys to stand up and move near me. As he approached, he eventually was close enough to be in the swing path of my arms. My mother illustrated that at the very point where his body entered my swing plane, I no longer had the right to swing my arms at will. My right to swing my arms ended where his right to not be struck began. Simple, but very effective, and burned into my memory.

It was her various responsibilities in this church that afforded me my first look at the innate wisdom my mother brought to bear. I am certain her wisdom, like all wisdom, was born of mistakes and miscues, but it just seemed to flow from her. I doubt I would have used this word as a pre-teen to describe one of her qualities, but looking back it is certainly fitting—admirable. My mother was admirable.

Along with my early observations of her positive influence on others, both young and old, I also began to notice how studious she was. As a Sunday School teacher, she took her job seriously and began preparations to teach her class for any Sunday morning the afternoon of the Sunday before. My mother would study at her desk, an old style wooden number that she bought at a thrift store and refinished in our garage. It had open shelves down both sides and one drawer in the middle for pencils, pens, rulers, and the like.

Mom was also the family accountant, and steno books full of the figures associated with budgeting paycheck to paycheck were always readily visible on top of her desk. She would use one sheet of the green spiral-bound paper per paycheck, and, oddly, she would never scribe the numbers on the lines but rather at about a forty-five-degree angle down and across the middle of the page. The income figure would head the column of numbers, with little minus signs adjacent to each bill due. If the payment was an estimate, the letters "est." would appear next to the number. She would always estimate high, thereby leaving hope of a little more discretionary income at the end of the month.

On the open shelves down each side of her desk were dozens of books, some quite hefty, mostly related to the study of Christianity. I remember a *Matthew Henry's Commentary* and a *William Barclay Commentary* and a handful of Bibles in different translations. One of her favorites, which she read through several times over the years, was Oswald Chambers's book, *My Utmost for His Highest*. This book is written in daily devotion style, and I have memories of her sitting at her desk, bent over the volume, carefully reading while touching the lines gently with her fingers, and then lifting her head, removing her reading glasses, and saying, more to herself than to anyone else, "Boy, he is deep!"

Perhaps it was her studious nature and her obvious commitment to the welfare of the church that facilitated her selection as a member of the pastor search committee. To my knowledge this was her first foray into this delicate adventure, designed to conclude with the selection of a pastor whom an entire congregation would respect and appreciate, but was definitely not her last. Mom believed that pastors received a calling, just like other professionals, and that a divinely called pastor would be married to a woman who was likewise called to serve the church. The result of hers and the other committee members' search on this particular occasion was a pastor-wife team who brought a level of sophistication, wisdom, and growth to our church.

Brother Robert Beal (not his real name) was a distinguished looking gentlemen in his early sixties, over six feet tall with huge hands and long feet that were accentuated by his lace-up brogans. From my angle in the congregation, when he sat in the pastor's chair to the right of the pulpit and crossed his legs, his shoe looked like the bottom of a water ski. He was a basso profondo and his voice, although never melodramatic, would resonate off the walls of the sanctuary. During the opening sentences of his sermon, he would always remove his wrist watch, folding the metal band to make the watch face angle up, visible to him, and set it on the pulpit just to the right of the flat surface. I don't know what it did for others, but it comforted me to see that it was at least his intent to end on time.

He preached with his flexibly bound Bible open to the scripture lesson and draped over the back of his left hand. It was also his custom to insert a very lengthy prayer into his order of worship. It was a challenge for me to keep my head bowed and eyes closed that long; so I would typically take a peek around at the people in the congregation and especially check on my mother from time to time, lest I be caught looking around. I remember her attractive profile as she lost herself in the prayer, head more erect than bowed, her eyes peacefully closed, never squeezed; as Brother Beal prayed she would slowly and rhythmically rub the bridge of her nose gently between her thumb and forefinger in short, half-inch, up and down motions.

41

Brother Beal's wife, whom I will call Rhonda, was a lovely, self-composed woman, also in her sixties. She was a trained mezzo-soprano, able to hit notes both in the tenors' range and in the sopranos' octave, and brought balance and depth to the choir.

Occasionally, the Sunday evening crowd (typically a much smaller group) would gather after services at the Beals' home for coffee, cake, and conversation. On one occasion, I remember Mom and me asking for an additional cup and then stepping into Ms. Rhonda's kitchen to get it. Ms. Rhonda spoke from the family room, "Kathryn, look in the cabinet to the right of the sink," but then in true southern hostess fashion, trailed her words by coming into the kitchen to ensure we found what we were looking for. When my mom opened the cabinet, a paper rabbit face about the size of an apple began to jiggle on its springy base attached to the inside of the cabinet door. The words printed near the rabbit's mouth were "You still shake me up." Mom and Ms. Rhonda locked eyes and shared a knowing laugh when she said demurely, "Oh, Robert put that there." I could tell my mother thought it wonderful that a husband would give such an affectionate gift to his wife after more than thirty-five years of marriage.

The music program at our church was wonderful. Christmas and Easter Cantatas and various musicals such as *South Pacific* were well prepared and executed and well attended. My father was a weekly feature on the back row in the tenor section, and it was in this church that my love for gospel music and tight four-part harmony was born. There were two or three gifted sopranos and altos who were only four or so years older than I, and I dreamed of one day being able to sing that same seemingly effortless alto.

The musical gene runs strong through my father's family. It barely walks through my mom's. On my father's side, I have aunts and uncles and cousins who can sing, play guitar, play violin, and one aunt, Deborah (ninth in the line-up of ten children), who can play a mean piano. I have wonderful memories over several decades of harmonizing with my dad, aunts, uncles, and cousins while Aunt Deborah played number after number from the *Baptist Hymnal*. In 2007, my first-cousin Brandon, sang the national anthem at a home game for the Birmingham Barons, the Double A affiliate of the Chicago White Sox. It just so happened to be Father's Day, and Dad and I were in attendance, as was Brandon's dad, Sam. Brandon represented the Collins clan quite admirably that day.

My mother loved all kinds of music, and just because she couldn't sing, it didn't keep her from wanting to sing. Many Saturday mornings when I was a child, she would come into my room and awaken me with a song called "Lazy Bones." She would sit on the side of my bed and sing, "Lazy bones, sleepin' in the sun. How do you expect to get your day's work done, hmmmmmm?" That little wake-up routine was simple; yet it served as a powerful signal that all was well in my world.

She loved for the two of us to sing together, which we did many, many times. It wasn't that she couldn't carry the melody line—it was just that when she changed verses, she sometimes changed keys. I thought we sounded nice together, much like related people do because their voices are genetically similar. She would sing the melody and I would provide harmony; but since she was apt to change keys at any break in a song, I had to stay on my musical toes, so to speak. When she inadvertently changed keys, I would always say with a giggle, "Mom, you changed keys," and she would always respond, "I did?"

We had a couple of songs that we sang together over and over and in so doing became quite accomplished with them. The song "He Touched Me" was our go-to spiritual favorite, and a whimsical song that Mom taught me entitled "I'm Goin' Back to Where (pronounced *whir*) I Come From" was our all-time favorite. This was a song about a country girl who decides to take the grand adventure to the big city. Upon her arrival in Kansas City, she meets a man who asks her if she'd "like to step around," and she answers, "Yeap, that's what I'm here for (pronounced *fir*)." Her response to his question was a spoken part and we had practiced together so many times that we had the inflection, the timing, and the countrified pronunciation down pat. In the song, the man ends up duping her out her fourteen dollars and skips town. After that betrayal, she decides "this city life just ain't no place for a gal like me to end in, so I'm goin' back to *whir* I come from." We sang that song together well into her seventies, and for some reason, it never failed to remind us how very much we loved each other.

The morning after Christmas 1967, I awoke to my mom sitting on the edge of my bed and smiling down lovingly at me. She then proceeded to tell me directly but gently that Santa Claus did not exist. We talked about the subject for several minutes, and I asked if the tooth fairy and the Easter Bunny fell into the same category. Mom verified that was indeed the case. I was okay with the news and in truth had probably reached the age where the physical and logistical challenges of Santa's mission had started to raise some doubts in my mind. Our conversation included a discussion of what normally happens on one's birthday. She said, "Honey, who gets presents on your birthday?" "Me," I answered. "And whose birthday is Christmas?" "Jesus'," I said. "That's right, honey," she said.

Months following that exchange, after Thanksgiving 1968, I saw for the first time (but not the last) the militant side of my mother. She launched a one-woman campaign against the commercialism of Christmas. We still gave gifts to each other and a few family members, such as my grandmothers and any babies in the family, but as far as decorating our house, having a tree—all that stopped. One year, she bought the spindliest pine tree she could find, and she probably broke a myriad of copyright laws as she hung one big glass ball on the tree, which bent it over, Charlie Brown style. Another year, she bought a styrofoam sign printed with the words "Seasons Greetings" and placed it in the middle of our front yard hoisted on a bent stick she had found in the woods behind our house. I heard her pontificate on the pressures that the commercialism of Christmas brought onto families. She would say, "A family spends more money than they have on Christmas gifts for everyone, and then spends the entire next year paying that bill off."

Sadly however, Mom was living in the proverbial glass house as she tossed those stones. She had expensive tastes, particularly in clothes, shoes, and cars, and sometimes her spending was a source of frustration for my father. There were also people in her life whom she could not resist buying for—her younger sister, Gail, being one. My aunt Gail and her husband, Gary, were a very successful couple and lacked for nothing, but that was not the point to my mother. My father would be disgusted with her when she spent more money than she should have on a gift for my aunt; it never seemed to faze my mother, however, as gift giving was an undeniable facet of her "love language" and she adored her baby sister.

Her love for nice cars was something she shared with my father. On their honeymoon, they drove their brand-spanking-new 1955 sky blue and white Chevy Bel Air hardtop to Miami, Florida. Knowing both of them, I imagine they enjoyed the head turns, just as I would have, as they drove slowly down Collins Avenue. While we lived in Titusville, my mother got a hankering for a Volkswagen Carmen Ghia, which my father somehow accommodated. It was cherry red and a convertible, and highly impractical as family transit, because I was growing like a weed and soon actually outgrew the backseat. My mother's dream car was a baby blue Lincoln Continental with the spare tire compartment situated in the middle of the trunk and visible as a body detail. She saw one for the first time parallel-parked in downtown Birmingham and thought it the most beautiful automobile she had ever lain eyes on. My father never managed to afford that one, however, opting years later to surprise her with as close a substitute as he could afford, a beautiful white Ford LTD, with a rich brown vinyl top and brown interior. I remember her being happy with the car, but not thrilled, and I felt sorry for my father.

Even though I was not a decision maker in my family scheme, that didn't mean I couldn't recognize bad ones. As long as I was under their roof, I remembered sensing friction. I would witness a conversation between the two of them and readily see how what one of them said had been misinterpreted by the other. This is no special gift; I believe all children have this ability. Unfortunately, children have neither the maturity nor the skill set to facilitate better communication between their parents; so for the vast majority of the twenty-eight years that my parents were married, as best I could tell, they misunderstood each other and never really communicated.

I remember a particularly fierce row that took place while the three of us were driving somewhere; our destination escapes my memory. What doesn't escape my memory is the fact that after several minutes of intense conversation, my father demanded to be let out of the car; my mother accommodated him. As she drove away, I peered after him through the back windshield; and as the figure of my father got smaller and smaller, I threw a panicked fit, begging my mother to go back and get my daddy. I remember seeing the anger melt away from her face like warm wax, and she quickly turned the car around and went back to collect him. In my eighteen years with them, I never questioned their love for me, but the substance of their feelings for each other remained a mystery.

My parents' shared mission of raising a child whose behavior would always be the source of compliments from friends and family continued in Titusville. The spankings for bad behavior ceased around the age of eleven and behavior modification began to come in different, more creative forms. One such lesson is as clear in my memory as if it had happened yesterday. After having been told, more than once, to pick up my clothes from the bathroom floor after bathing and failing to ingrain that habit, I came in from play one day and saw my favorite shorts and shirt lying on top of the kitchen garbage. I was shocked when I saw them there; and my father, who had lain in wait for my reaction, said, "I mean it, either pick up your clothes or I will throw them away." That did the trick, at least for that bad habit.

My parents also realized the value of experiential learning, and as long as my actions wouldn't lead to any bodily harm, they would give me my head, so to speak. I recall two such lessons. The first was my determination to cure a case of hiccups, using orange juice instead of water with the "hold your breath and take ten swallows method." We were at the breakfast table when the aggravating spasms struck me, and I thought ten swallows of the delicious orange juice would be far more satisfying that ten swallows of water. Both parents warned me that too much juice would be rough on my stomach, but I insisted and they let me go. On the third round of treatment, the acid in the juice had taken its toll and I was "green around the gills." The second bitter lesson, and I do mean bitter, was my insistence on eating a piece of the baking chocolate I had found in the cupboard. It smelled so good; so I ask my mother if I could have a piece. She warned that it would not taste as good as it smelled because there was no sugar in it. But I continued to trust my nose more than my mother and hounded her for permission to try a square. She finally relented, and I ran head-long into my own willfulness—the chocolate was horrible.

I had certain Saturday morning chores that had to be completed before I was allowed to go outside and play with my friends. If I focused on the tasks at hand, I could be finished in two hours, tops; but if I allowed myself to become distracted, the morning would slip away, and with it precious playtime. Occasionally, following a blown morning, I would attempt to negotiate with my mother in some fashion, but she never budged. I soon learned I had no one to blame but myself; the list of chores had not been lengthened, nor had Mom changed the rules.

I also had the responsibility to clean the kitchen after our meals on the weekend, and sometimes my propensity to procrastinate put me in much the same spot as when I frittered away a Saturday morning dilly-dallying around instead of completing my chores. Mom gave helpful instruction along the way such as "just back your ears and dive in," in other words, just get it over with. Her definition of neatness was so logical as to make it irrefutable. She would say, "Everything has a place, and everything in its place makes for a neat home."

My mother rarely became angry in these instances of my failure to yield gracefully to the established rules because she knew the boundaries had been set, and if I chose to spend all day doing something that should only take minutes, then that was my choice. Although painful, in a juvenile sense of that word, I learned the value of self-discipline during those tug-of-war days of pre-pubescent orneriness. It was not until my early teenage years however (those years that I suspect most parents lie awake at night in confusion) that my behaviors were occasionally the match to her short fuse. I remember only a couple of times when she totally lost her temper with me, but I cannot for the life of me remember the circumstances. I am certain of one thing however; the provocation occurred because I stepped over a line that my mother had clearly drawn and communicated.

When I was about twelve years old, I witnessed an epic display of her temper. At the time, I was mortified by her behavior, but as I matured I began to view the circumstances of that day with a degree of pride. It all occurred by chance, really. Mom and I were in our car and stopped along with four other cars behind a yellow school bus offloading a group of middle-schoolers. The bus had its STOP flapper appropriately extended when suddenly a car passed all five cars and the school bus, made a left turn, and drove quickly away. My mother was apoplectic. With lips set in a tight line, she instructed me to watch where that car went. As soon as the school bus signaled the all clear, we were in hot pursuit. While she stared a hole through the windshield, I begged her to just let him go; but I might as well have been talking to a wall for all the good it did. We followed him to the drug store adjacent to the bowling alley in a strip mall across the street from our subdivision. She parked in the first empty space she saw and with single-minded purpose got out of the car and headed into the drug store. I literally had to jog to keep up with her and tried one more time to calm her down before she entered the store, to no avail. She walked down the center aisle, looking left and right, and eventually headed for the back of the drug store where there were several booths and a long soda fountain bar with a half-dozen round red vinyl-covered stools permanently affixed to the floor along its length. I peeked out from behind one of the display counters and saw him about the same time she did. He was sitting at one of the booths, his back to the wall and one leg stretched out down the length of the booth seat. He was young, self-absorbed, and appeared to be totally engrossed in a magazine. I held my breath. My mother drew herself up to her full five feet eight inches and leaned over the table, hands splayed on the tabletop, looked straight at him, and said, "Do you mean to tell me that you passed that line of cars and that school bus and endangered the lives of those children so you could come here and read a magazine!" with her voice rising in pitch and volume throughout the accusation. His eyes registered shock, and his eyebrows registered fear as my mother took him to task for his unbridled recklessness. The only thing he could manage was a contrite sounding, "Yes, ma'am." I have told this story to friends and family a dozen times, and all of the listeners who actually knew my mother found it totally believable, shaking their heads gently up and down in affirmation, smiling and giggling with every added detail.

My family lore is rich with stories of my mom and her temperament. My grandmother, trying to provide support and advice during Mom's third and only full-term pregnancy, is remembered as having said, "If Kathryn ever gets pregnant again, I am leaving the country." I am certain the hormonal changes typical in a pregnancy didn't help matters.

Once, before I was born, and in the early years of their marriage, my mom and dad were having dinner with his family in my grandparents' large southern home in Thorsby, Alabama. My father was one of ten, situated number five in the line-up with his younger siblings ranging in age from two to sixteen when my parents married in 1955. As the story goes, Royce, the youngest of the children, was repetitively demanding a piece of pie and accentuating his demands by rhythmically banging the end of his fork on the table. My mother gave him the evil eye in an attempt to administer a little silent behavior modification. My uncle, only about four at the time, called her out by asking why she was looking at him "like a fool." Mom recalled wishing she could have either slid under the table or disappeared altogether.

Nothing could get under my mother's skin quicker than a discourteous driver. If a driver was traveling too fast for the conditions or exceeding the speed limit or changing lanes in a reckless way, he would no doubt provoke my mother to wrath. When we bought a new car, the first thing she wanted to find was the horn. She used it to express herself; the longer the honk, the worse the offense. In the late 1980s the term "road rage" entered our American lexicon; and early on, not realizing its full meaning, I innocently used it to tease my mother. I used to tell her that when she went to heaven, God was going to put her on a five-mile-long circular highway and then allow all manner of temptation to confront her in the form of speeders, inconsiderate lane changers, and the like. Once she had completed her tenth lap in a row without losing her cool, then and only then would God illuminate the off-ramp to the pearly gates. She, of course, would giggle each time I said this. I used this silly tease in my mother's eulogy and added that, for all I knew, she was still circling. I knew Mom would appreciate the humor.

My mom's road rage could only be defined in the very lightest sense of the term, as she would never have used her automobile to put anyone in danger or harm them. But yet, as stories of full-blown road rage began to gain national attention, I feared for her safety on the road. Thankfully, I was an adult in the late 1980s and I told her, in no uncertain terms woman-to-woman, that she simply had to stop expressing her anger at other drivers when they failed to meet her driving standards. To the best of my knowledge, she yielded to my direction. The stories of people being shot during such altercations went a long way in convincing her also, I am certain.

As I recall and then examine the myriad stories of my mother's temperament, I can see a pattern. Certainly not always, but many times her very keen sense of right and wrong was at the forefront, sort of a righteous anger, if you will. Perhaps it was a bit overdeveloped, but my mom was the kind of patriot you wanted on your team if you were ever wronged or mistreated.

Thankfully though, when it came to raising me, she displayed a great deal of wisdom before "jumping to my defense." I can remember coming in from play, breathless with indignation over some playground fracas where I felt I had been mistreated, and telling her the details of my friends' infractions. At the end of my diatribe, she would ask, without exception, "Well, what did you do?" The answer to that question never failed to lend perspective and usually led to a much clearer picture of what had actually transpired between us kids. Once again, my mother used these opportunities to teach me. These were the days where the concept of self-awareness began to take hold in my mind: in other words, understanding that my behavior affected the behavior of others, both negatively and positively. These early lessons were also the foundation for my understanding that there was always more to a story. Understanding there were always two sides, and sometimes three or four sides, to a story helped me immensely during my career as a supervisor and later a manager, but also benefited me many times in my personal life. Finally, understanding that what was revealed at first blush would always be shy of the whole truth also led to an appreciation of the supreme worth of patience. I learned its value early and have been fighting the uphill battle to gain it ever since.

Much in the same fashion as a coach who used to play the game but found that he was a much better teacher of the game than a player, my mom guided me over my formative years to an understanding of the destructive power of words, especially words spoken in anger. Through my mother's self-awareness and her study of Scripture, she knew that being short-tempered was in direct conflict with the fruits of the Spirit. She thoroughly understood the command to "bridle one's tongue" even though sometimes she struggled mightily to do it.

Another area of my mother's life in which she struggled to maintain self-control but taught me better was her appetite for food, especially sweets. Upon returning to her job at the phone company in Texas shortly after my birth, she carried me cradled in her arms to see her friends there. She recounted that one of her friends took me into her own arms, looked down at me, and said, "Honey, I just knew you were going to come out looking like a Hershey bar." Apparently, Hershey bars were Mom's "pickles and ice cream" during her pregnancy.

She just loved to eat, and especially loved to eat out. With my father on second shift at the Kennedy Space Center, working from 2:00 p.m. until 11:00 p.m., she and I would often venture out for dinner. She loved barbecue with the sweet red sauce, and a local restaurant called Fat Boy's was our go-to favorite. Also in our dining-out circuit was Lum's, on Highway 1 across from the Indian River, featuring hotdogs steamed in beer, and an Italian place (whose name I cannot recall) near the church that specialized in calzones. We ate at this place so often that the owner/cook added a child-sized calzone to his menu because I could never finish a regular-sized one. But the crème de la crème of main courses for my mom was fried shrimp; the sweet meat surrounded by the crunchy batter, followed by a nibble from a good hushpuppy, would just send her into orbit. She also loved fish, the abundance of both fish and shrimp being another perk of living on the Atlantic coast. When she ate seafood, she craved beer. She rarely gave in to this temptation, however, feeling that as a Sunday School teacher she should not drink it, as it would set a bad example if she were ever to be observed by a member of her class. She called it "avoiding all appearances of evil." Occasionally though, under the cover of an entirely different city and state, she would succumb.

For my mom, anytime was dessert time. Anything chocolate was of primary interest, but she also loved strawberry shortcake, watermelon, banana pudding (the cooked-over-the-stove kind), and pecan pie. We knew exactly where to go to get the dessert we wanted. The Dairy Queen, just outside of our Florida subdivision and down the road about a mile, was the place to go for a hot fudge sundae with nuts. The bread store, about a half a mile closer, was the location of the gold-foil wrapped Chunky's that we loved. (Not the silver ones you find today, but the gold ones—I have not seen them in years.) If a pecan log or pecan turtles was our craving, then Stuckey's was our destination. She loved Circus Peanuts, an orange colored marshmallow affair shaped like a huge peanut, and Orange Slices, basically an out-sized orange jelly bean coated in sugar and shaped like an orange slice. These orange delights could be purchased practically anywhere. I remained amazed that dozens of years later she could walk down the aisle of a convenience store after visiting the restroom and, even with macular degeneration, could readily spot these orange slices hanging on a peg. If we were craving either banana pudding or pecan pie, we would, quite honestly, have to settle because no one made banana pudding like my maternal grandmother, Lucy, and no one made pecan pie like my paternal grandmother, Alta.

In her later years, while living in Alabama, Mom added Waffle House, Cracker Barrel, and McDonald's to her list of favorite restaurants. In 2004 it was her compulsion to eat at these places that offered me the first clues that something was amiss and that her judgment was not what it had been. From that perspective, I am thankful that something she had loved to do for her entire life, sit down at a restaurant and enjoy a meal, had not lessened as she aged.

Breakfast was her favorite meal, and I can still see her sitting across from me at the booth of a Waffle House taking her first careful sip of a hot cup of black coffee and saying, "That's so good; I like my coffee like I like my men, dark and hot." I knew it was coming but got tickled anyway, every time. Her normal "eating out" breakfast would consist of something sweet such as pancakes or a waffle, followed by something not sweet like two eggs over-easy or a few strips of bacon. Although she loved the sweet taste, she never wanted that to be the last flavor in her mouth, always choosing to "cut the sweet" with something salty.

Throughout my life, my mother and I have eaten out hundreds of times together, and I marvel how through such an ordinary activity she was able to provide a worthy example of how to treat people who were, for at least an hour or so, subservient to you. My mother's treatment of the numerous waiters and waitresses whom she and I encountered over the years made strong and lasting impressions on me. She always treated them in a very respectful manner, always tipped fairly, and, believing it to be the sweetest sound to the human ear, always called them by their name.

My mother was, overall, a very good cook, including baking, but her specialty was making candy. My mom's fudge and divinity were the stuff of legends and were heralded on both sides of my family as the best gifts one could receive from Aunt Kakki. Mom would frequently cook up a batch of either fudge or divinity and give it as a Christmas gift to some of my cousins. I can readily recall my cousin Donna clutching the box with the tag that read, "To Donna, From Aunt Kakki," in both hands, closing her eyes, wishing the contents to be my mom's fudge, then opening it and seeing to her delight that her wish had come true. She wouldn't even risk setting the box down, but with a little squeal of happiness she would head off somewhere to hide the goody so that she and her precious husband, Kenny, could enjoy it later in the privacy of their bedroom, out of sight from their three children.

The recipes for both fudge and divinity are extremely difficult to master. The weather has to be right, the humidity has to be right, and they have to be cooked to exactly the right temperature. The divinity has to be cooked until an inserted spoon draws a hair-thin string of mixture when removed. The fudge has to be cooked until a very small amount of the mixture forms a "soft ball" when dropped into cold water and then "flattens when removed." The Hershey's fudge recipe actually gives a disclaimer saying basically, "This recipe is hard; so don't even try it if you aren't a really good cook." Yet my mother could make both of these recipes and hit on them virtually every time without using a candy thermometer nor any other special cookware; she just had the touch. If I was around during the making of the candies, she would always give me the opportunity to "lick the bowl." I never took up the offer for the divinity, but scraping the warm leftover fudge from the pan Mom had used, putting the spoon into my mouth upside down, and allowing the rich, sweet, smooth chocolate to slowly melt away on my tongue was unadulterated bliss.

Looking back, I think Mom would have been classified as an emotional eater and probably found a lot of comfort in food. A slim 147 pounds when she married my father, she allowed her weight to creep up to over 200 pounds over the years. My mother was tall and large boned and carried the weight well, but it was certainly taking its toll on her back, which she had injured playing softball in her twenties, and her vital organs as the excess fat and sugar slowly exacted their cost. I saw her struggle over the years to bring this passion under control. She tried a myriad of diets and would from time to time drop thirty or forty pounds, but her old habits would always eventually catch up to her and the weight would reappear over time. She knew she should take action, but just like the alcoholic who knows better but drinks anyway, she sought refuge in food. Her coaching for me consisted of confessions over her unwillingness to challenge the weight gain when it was small. She recalled gaining the first ten pounds after marrying and saying to herself, "I don't look bad at this weight." Then the next ten pounds was gained and again she said to herself, "I don't look bad at this weight." Gaining a little weight and then justifying it as "not so bad" was the pattern that eventually resulted in over seventy pounds of total gain. Once again, through her self-awareness and her familiarity with Scripture she knew her self-control in this area was coming up short but could not seem to get a permanent handle on it. Having the genetic propensity from both sides of my family to be heavy, I have treasured her guidance through the years—a little at a time, left unchecked, equals a lot over time.

My father would tease my mother unmercifully about her weight; and I would like to believe he thought that approach would help her, but it most certainly did not. I remember one occasion, in the early 1980s when my husband and I were visiting my parents at their home, when my father's teasing went way over the line. It had gotten late and my mother had gone to bed and my husband and I stayed up to visit with my father. I cannot even recall why the subject of Mom's appetite came up in conversation, but my father began to do a grotesque and cruel imitation of my mother eating at a recent church social. I was so offended and so hurt by his insensitivity toward my beloved mother that had I been his son as opposed to his daughter I probably would have struck him. Instead, I stormed out of the house, slamming the door so hard as to jar the hanging pictures crooked. I just started walking down the dirt road in the dark, too angry to think straight, until my husband came trotting after me, offering his comfort. I recognized my mother's weakness for food, and I also recognized the toll it was taking on her health, but I believed the best approach to help her involved support, not ridicule.

Prior to my mom marrying, she had often babysat children and was very good with little people. She participated in activities with them and was a firm believer that children interpreted your love for them as you spent time with them. I heard her say a million times, "Love to a child is spelled 't-i-m-e.'" In Titusville, while his mother worked, she babysat a little boy whom I will call Robbie. We all dearly loved that little boy. He was a beautiful child with very blond hair and very blue eyes and a terrific demeanor. I remember feeling the first unfamiliar pangs of jealousy over Mom's affection for Robbie. It actually came to a head one day as I acted out in childlike fashion to get her attention and was sent home to my room. We lived just across the street from Robbie, and as I trudged home I began practicing almost immediately what I would say to her when she finally came into my room to address the situation. My plan consisted of manufacturing some tears and then telling her I thought she loved Robbie more than she loved me. As an adult, when I recall this planned scene between us, I realize now she had several response options available to her. For one, she could have told me to stop being childish (I was five years older than Robbie) and to wipe those alligator tears away. Or she could have punished me for acting out, or ignored me, or told me not to be silly and thereby not acknowledging my underlying feelings of jealousy. But she chose none of those. Even though I am quite certain she knew I was trying to play her, throwing out the "you love him more than me" card, she didn't rise to the bait. Instead, she took me in her arms and told me how much she loved me and that her love for me would never, ever change. I think her response was brilliant. I was being a brat because I was jealous; and instead of making me feel worse, she reassured me, and in so doing modified my future behavior in similar situations for the better.

The year 1971 marked the completion of my first six years of school. I had been at Imperial Estates Elementary for four grades, third through sixth, and had learned a lot more than just the basics of science, history, social studies, and math. I was growing up and beginning to take notice of things and people around me—particularly people who were not like me—and naturally sought my mother's wisdom in how to accept and deal with them. In the fifth grade, there was a particularly boisterous male student who delighted in picking on me.

My mother suggested that she and I visit his home and have a talk with him and his parents—which is exactly what we did—end of problem. In 1970 African-American students began to be bused to Imperial Estates Elementary, and one girl, named Rose, emerged as athletic competition for me. I could run faster than any girl in sixth grade until Rose showed up. Rose had strabismus, a vision condition in which a person cannot align both eyes simultaneously under normal conditions, and was by my observation probably not as well off as I was. I also sensed some minor hostility from Rose in the beginning, but over time I befriended her, under the influence of my mother's graciousness.

When I was in the fifth grade, there was a sixth-grade girl who had a condition that caused her eyes to bulge noticeably. My mother helped me see her as no different from any other child. Between my mother and my best friend, Joyce, who had the kindest heart for people born with physical or mental challenges, I had wonderful examples of what compassion and sensitivity really looked like.

Joyce and I matriculated to seventh grade in September 1971 and attended Andrew Jackson Junior High, which was located across town, several miles from our homes. We finally learned what it was like to stand on the street corner to catch a school bus every morning around 6:30 a.m. We could now empathize with the African-American students who had been bused to our grammar school a few years earlier as a result of a Federal Court mandate. The forced busing was designed to achieve racial balance in elementary and secondary educational institutions across the South, which was a good thing; but having to rise so early to catch that bus was probably not a lot of fun.

As it is with anyone entering their teens, I faced the multitude of changes and challenges, including puberty, which seemed to arrive in droves. It was around this time that I realized there was at least one subject my mother was not totally comfortable talking about with me—sex. She tiptoed around the subject, and when I turned twelve she bought me a book entitled *Almost Twelve,* which covered the subject in enough detail for me to realize that one moment's indiscretion with a member of the opposite sex could have life altering consequences. On the day I was first visited by the "curse" (and whoever first used that description had to know there was no better term in the English language to describe it), she was there for me, as always, and introduced me to the medieval contraptions that had to have been the onus of all women of her generation. I remember feeling as if my life had taken an unalterable turn and felt it totally unfair that boys had no equivalent to the physical discomfort and sheer inconvenience of the whole female process with which to deal. Mom assured me I would survive, and that soon it would become a totally manageable occurrence. Of course, she was right. I did however carry on some of her Victorian tendencies, not so much with the subject of sex, but with the subject of the "curse." And for years to come, when shopping for the necessary items, I would ensure they were buried at the bottom of the grocery cart underneath a pile of other purchases so they could not be easily seen. I would go so far as building a little cereal box and milk carton fortress around the offending products as they rode the conveyor to the cashier!

I have fairly clear memories of my junior high school experiences; and aside from being introduced to an entirely new set of classmates and having to adapt to the new hierarchy, I noticed that our teachers were no longer just asking us to memorize and then recite back this fact or that equation. They were asking us to express ourselves and share freely with the class what we thought and how we felt. I got my first taste of having to uphold something I didn't support when I was placed on the pro-smoking side of a debate team and had to defend the merits of free-will smoking. My mother rolled her eyes a bit when I shared the details of this assignment with her, seeing the irony, as did I—we had been encouraging my father for years to stop smoking. She thought I would be a good debater, however, having accused me from time to time over the years of being able to "argue with a sign post."

Most prominently, I remember my junior high school years as the backdrop for two learnings from my mother that had a profound impact on my life. The first presented itself in the form of an assignment from my seventh-grade social studies teacher. We were told to create a project that would illustrate some important historical achievement that held significance for a certain society. I chose to build a model of the Parthenon out of Popsicle sticks, styrofoam, and glue, as we had recently studied Ancient Greece and I had become familiar with the temple erected for the goddess Athena when the Athenian Empire was at the height of its power. As engaged parents, my mother and my father gave helpful advice but wisely left the bulk of the project to me. I enjoyed the challenge and every afternoon would go to the work space my father had sectioned off for me in our garage and work on it.

On the day the projects were due, we brought our masterpieces into the cafeteria as instructed and set them up on the tables. We were told that our grades would be given that evening and would be available for us to see the following morning. I remember excitedly walking over to my Popsicle stick Parthenon the next morning and to my horror seeing a big fat C adjacent to it. I was mortified. That C stood for catastrophe in my mind, and I felt tears begin to form in my eyes. To that point, I had never received anything lower than a B on any school assignment, and in my young mind I was now, clearly, a failure and a disappointment to my parents. The tendency toward perfectionism that had been slyly shaping me over the last several years was now a fully realized problem that had to be dealt with. When I got home that afternoon, I sought guidance and solace from my mother. She asked two questions. First, she asked me if I knew why I had received a C. I told her, "No, ma'am. I don't know why." She advised that I respectfully ask my teacher why I had received an average grade and explain to him that I wanted to know so I could do better next time.

Her second question was a simple one back in 1972, but grew broader and more important and more meaningful as I aged. She asked, "Did you do your best?" I answered, "Yes, ma'am, I did my best." "That's all a mule can do, is his best," she said. I nodded my head in understanding, tears of relief flowing down my cheeks.

Perhaps that statement sounds odd to someone not familiar with farm life or farm animals—so I will explain. A mule is a noble beast of burden. It is a hybrid cross between a female horse and a male donkey, typically not prepotent—in other words, sterile. Prior to farm mechanization, mules played a vital role in aiding the farmer as he readied his field for planting, pulling the plowshare through the earth, row after row, attuned to the "gee" and the "haw" of his master's voice. Mules are extremely durable and extremely strong and benefit from the hybrid vigor or superior qualities that, more often than not, arise from the crossbreeding of genetically different animals. Mules give their master everything they have, day in and day out; but like all of creation, they have their limits. That's what my mother was talking about—just do your best—that's all you can do, is your best.

I took my mother's advice and respectfully asked my social studies teacher to share with me the key components to my C grade. He said primarily it was a lack of creativity; I immediately flashed back to the cafeteria tables filled with projects and then remembered the numerous Parthenons that I had seen. "Okay," I thought to myself, "that makes sense." Later that afternoon, I shared the revelation with Mom, and she said, "Good, now you know." The following year the same assignment was given, and I decided to construct the tomb of Jesus. My dad suggested I use chicken wire to actually form it, and my mom suggested papier-mâché to cover it. It was unique and well-researched and afforded me a no-tears B+.

The second life lesson I learned against the backdrop of junior high school was, in totality, to be myself. I should amend this statement by explaining that what I actually learned was what an important concept this was, but knowing what to do and actually becoming proficient at it often occur years apart, as was the case with me in learning to be who I was. I was well into my fifties before the balm of being one's self finally began to soothe my tired mind. But perhaps it would have taken even longer had it not been for the events leading up to my eighth-grade class picture and the foundational learning my mother pulled from it.

The moniker "Plain Jane" is a most fitting description of my physical appearance in junior high school. I was tall and shapeless. I wore dark-rimmed glasses and a removable retainer to close a sizable gap between my front teeth (inherited from my father). I also had a juvenile hairstyle, parted on one side, shoulder length, and held behind one ear with a multi-colored barrette that Mom and I had purchased from the Five and Dime. I had not noticed my appearance as anything but normal prior to junior high school. But that soon changed as the girls at Jackson were much more mature than I. Their young bodies, more developed and their appearances more sophisticated, albeit manufactured, stood out in sharp contrast. By the eighth grade, I had upgraded to wire rimmed glasses; the retainer had done its job and the gap between my front teeth had closed; and I was sporting the same hairstyle of the vast majority of girls at the school, long and parted in the middle. But I was still foolishly chasing some illusive image. I had noticed one girl in particular who had, what I judged to be, a lovely smile. She had a way of spreading her top lip across her big white teeth, and I thought it worthy of emulation; so for eighth-grade school pictures I attempted to replicate her smile.

The photos were awful. When I took them home, my mother simply asked, "What were you doing with your upper lip?" And my father commented, "Honey, your mouth looks like a mule eating saw briers." I finally came clean with my mother, and in her wonderful way of handling me, she said, "But you have a great smile; why would you want someone else's smile?" "Great question," I thought. That was the foundational lesson for me, and a few years later my mother modified it in a most magnificent way.

As a dating teenager, when I was getting dressed for some social event, I would ask my mother rapid-fire, "Mom, does my hair look okay?" "Does this blouse match these pants?" "Should I wear these shoes?" "Are you sure I look all right?" She would always respond, "Yes, baby, you look wonderful; now, forget yourself, and loose yourself in other people." There it is. Definitely in the top three most important things I have ever learned—"be yourself" morphed into "forget yourself, and loose yourself in other people." I have found over the years that when I focus on others I am always, afterward, edified and joyful. I wouldn't trade anything for this knowledge, and I owe its origin to an awful eighth-grade class picture that my mother simply couldn't make sense of.

Following the final manned moon landing of Apollo 17 in December 1972, the Apollo program began to wind down, and employee layoffs began in earnest. It would be twelve more months before my father would receive his pink slip from the Bendix Corporation, but it finally happened, and in late 1973 we made plans to return to Alabama.

Our years in Florida had naturally been transformative for me as I aged from a second-grader to a ninth-grader. My relationship with my mother had been transformative as well. At almost fifteen years of age, I was becoming mature enough to look back at the multitude of experiences with her and categorize them, not with the specific intent to put the experiences into this bucket or that, but rather as a natural part of growing up, beginning to make my own interpretations. In so doing, a much more complex picture of her emerged—no less loving and no less loved, but certainly more realistic.

She was clearly still a heroic figure in my mind: doing whatever needed to be done, solving whatever problem I was faced with. Some of those events are hilarious in the re-telling—like the time she took the garden hose away from my gagging father to rinse away the fresh dog manure that had squished between my little two-year-old toes and was causing me to gag as well; or the time she grabbed the broom to chase the mouse that had treed my father and me on top of the washing machine. Some of the events are poignant—like the time she bent over the hospital bed allowing me to wrap my little arms around her neck for more than an hour while the nurses packed me in ice to lower my 104-degree body temperature. Or the time she managed to keep her composure, and thereby allowed me to keep mine, when she saw me walking toward her, my little dress soaked with blood from a kindergarten playground accident that had split the back of my head open. Most of the events however were far less dramatic, but no less meaningful to me, like rescuing me from embarrassment by coming up with a last minute birthday gift—a potato pig—an Irish potato with quarters stuck in for feet, dimes stuck in for ears and a tail, and a nickel stuck in for a snout.

I began to understand more clearly her paradoxical nature, seeing her kindness juxtaposed with her temper, and her playfulness juxtaposed with her stoicism. I saw her generosity and her desire for finery lead to predictable arguments with my father, and for the first time I was able to comprehend her vulnerabilities and her weaknesses.

My mother's halo had tilted a bit; but her imperfections and her humanness were signals that perhaps she needed me as much as I needed her. During our first fifteen years together the loving bond between us spread out in multi-dimensional layers and was made all the stronger by the complexities of it.

3

I remember that my parents chose to be together when they delivered the news to me that my father had been laid off from the Cape and that we would be returning to Alabama. My mother told me she had expected me to be very sad about the change; but when I examined my feelings about the upcoming re-location, I found I was actually looking forward to it. I believe it was she who taught me how to gracefully accept change, and perhaps even to anticipate it. She believed that everything happened for a reason, and that no matter how chaotic life seemed to appear, God was still in control and wanted the best for his children. "Things have a way of working out," she would declare. If she or my father had any reservations about leaving Florida, I was unaware of them; so, during the Christmas break of my ninth-grade year, we packed up and headed north—home, I guess one could say.

I knew I would miss my friend Joyce very much but believed in my heart we would always stay connected regardless of the miles between us. She had, likely unbeknownst to her and not fully realized by me until years later, been a very positive influence on me. She loved to read and was in a tie with my mother for the most compassionate person I have ever known. It was Joyce who taught me you could travel the world and step backward and forward in time through books; and it was Joyce, as my contemporary, who helped me understand that people who didn't look like me, smell like me, walk or talk like me, were no less "fearfully and wonderfully made." Looking over my shoulder out the rear window at the figure of my precious friend, growing smaller and smaller, standing on the sidewalk, waving goodbye, is my last clear memory of Titusville.

As we began our trek, my father did not have the promise of a job, but did have a small severance that he felt would keep us afloat until he found one. I am certain he was nervous about the future, but he was so gifted that we knew he would find a job relatively quickly and then everything would be back to normal for us. For reasons unknown to me, the majority of vacations and holidays up to that time had been spent with my mother's side of the family, either in Birmingham or Pensacola. In retrospect, this return to Alabama was good for all three of us because it afforded each of us, in different ways, important opportunities to either connect or re-connect with beloved members of my father's side of the family.

During the time my father was job-hunting, my parents and I lived in a rented two bedroom duplex in a tiny south-central Alabama town. Our duplex was adjacent to a main thoroughfare that meandered through the heart of several small towns, including Thorsby (my father's hometown).

My new school was mere walking distance from our duplex. There, I finished my ninth-grade year; but unlike Florida, which had a junior high school system where seventh, eighth and ninth graders attended classes together, I was now attending classes with sophomores, juniors, and seniors. A classic late-bloomer, I once again quickly judged myself to be much less sophisticated and therefore somewhat inferior to my new classmates. In a minor panic, I struggled to pick up my social and emotional developmental pace and catch up to my new group of friends. My mother exerted no pressure whatsoever on me to "speed up" but seemed content in the knowledge that my youthful awkwardness would naturally transform in its own good time. Thankfully, her instincts and her wisdom were there on more than one occasion to save me from myself during my "two steps forward and one step backward" journey into young adulthood.

One such rescue goes thus. I was not allowed to date until I turned sixteen, which in retrospect was still too young for me; but when I was fifteen, and the new girl in school, I had managed to catch the eye of a senior boy whom I will call Todd. Todd's attention flattered me immensely, but in all honesty he probably saw me more as untested prey than anything else. One of Todd's closest friends was another senior whom I will call Rick, and Rick had a keen interest in another freshman, a beautiful fifteen-year-old girl for whom I will use the name Cassie. Cassie and I were mere acquaintances, but I enjoyed being around her in the shameless hope that her good looks and sophistication would somehow rub off on me. In due time, through the supposedly foolproof machinations that seem to be a teenager's blind spot, a plan was hatched to get Cassie and me alone for a time on a Friday night with Rick and Todd. Step one of the plan consisted of me requesting permission for a sleepover at Cassie's house. Once ensconced, she and I would invent some reason to go out. We would then meet Rick and Todd at the prearranged time and location. As the fateful Friday loomed ever closer, I "paused on the banks of the Rubicon" and realized I could not lie to my mother—and, oh, how I wish this story had ended on that noble note; but it didn't. You see, I wanted to have my cake and eat it too; so I decided I would attempt to trade my honesty about the plan for her permission to go—it did not work. She listened attentively as I laid out the sordid details of our plan; and then she looked down at the floor, shook her head gently from side to side, and simply said, "No." She thanked me for being honest with her, but again gave a simple "No." My mother had dated a lot of men up until she married at age twenty-eight. Over the years, she had fended off multiple unsolicited advances from in-law uncles, friends of the family, and supervisors. She was therefore quite knowledgeable of how the male brain operated and simply could not, in good conscience, allow her vulnerable, inexperienced fifteen-year-old to put herself in that situation. I think subconsciously I was terribly relieved by her decision; so when I shared my story of truth-letting with my friends and they looked at me as if I had sprouted horns, it was a judgment I could tolerate.

One good thing that occurred while I was attending this small rural high school was that my Physical Education teacher saw that I had some amount of talent with a softball and invited me to try out for the slow-pitch traveling softball team of which she was a member. During the summers this team competed with other organized slow-pitch teams across the state, sometimes playing weekend tournaments away from home. Fortunately, I made the team and became the starting left fielder in the summer of 1974. My father really enjoyed coming to my games, and I loved having him there. My mother saw this as an opportunity for quality father-daughter time so she typically would not attend.

I also had my first paying job in the summer of 1974, and to be honest, it was that job that helped me come to the definitive conclusion that I would indeed go to college. My job was to assist in grading specimens of fruit as they passed me on a conveyor belt headed for the packers downstream. Any specimen that was rotten or too green or wormy had to be culled and pulled off the conveyor. I remember the timing of a particular softball tournament interfering with one scheduled shift of my fruit-grading job; so I asked my mom if she would fill in for me. My sweet mother agreed to help me out, thinking to herself, "How hard could it be to look at a piece of fruit and decide whether or not it looked good enough to eat?" When Dad and I returned from the tournament later that evening, Mom met me in the hallway and said these words, "Never again!" She then related the story of her day at the fruit barn. As the specimens were approaching, she would deliberate as to whether one needed to be culled, and by the time she had made up her mind the offending fruit was out of reach. Routinely, the conveyor belt would halt and someone on the end would yell back up the line, "Somebody's lettin' bad fruit go!" Mom said she had no doubt who the "somebody" was. She had me so tickled. It reminded both of us of our all-time favorite episode of "I Love Lucy" where Lucy and Ethel tried in vain to wrap all of the chocolate candy coming their way on a similar conveyor.

During our short stay in the duplex, while Dad continued his job hunt, I would occasionally spend time with my paternal grandmother, affectionately known as Big Momma. It must have been her capacity for hard work that earned her that nickname, because it couldn't have been her physical stature. Standing only five feet tall and never weighing more than 120 pounds soaking wet, she was the only daughter and the eldest in a family of seven siblings. The Collins family lore suggests that when she met and married my grandfather on December 2, 1923, at the ripe old age of seventeen, her father practically disowned her, not able to come to grips with his baby girl marrying a boy from a different county. To him, it was the equivalent of "running off."

After my grandparents wed, they proceeded to start a family of their own rather quickly. The first of their ten children, my aunt Lula Mae, was born in 1924, and over the next twenty-nine years they continued to have children, culminating with the birth of my uncle Royce in 1953. My grandmother could have well been the author of the saying, "A woman's work is never done."

My grandfather, known as Big Daddy, a name indeed descriptive of his stature, passed away from a massive heart attack over his first cup of coffee the morning of April 1,1968. Upon hearing the news, my parents and I began the eight-hour trek from Titusville to Thorsby to attend his funeral. I wondered, apparently out loud, if the news of my grandfather's passing could be some sort of April Fool's joke. My mother gently assured me that an event of such a serious nature would never be the subject of a prank.

When we arrived after the long sad trip, I noticed the crepe myrtles, planted across the front property line of my grandparents' lot, their graceful branches green and arched, had not yet revealed their pinkish blooms. My father parked our car in front of the "big house" between two of the crepe myrtles and for several seconds after shutting down the engine, nothing happened. I watched them in silence from the back seat, much like a spectator at a tennis match, as my parents simply looked at each other, likely gathering themselves for the multitude of emotional interactions to come.

The "big house," near the heart of downtown Thorsby, was a large plantation-styled home on a sprawling lot that my grandparents and some of the younger children had lived in for the last ten years, the eldest five children and the in-laws having chipped in to purchase the house back in 1958. As a child, primarily during our holiday visits, I spent many fun-filled hours exploring the expansive grounds, often trying to coax the cats to come up onto the front porch swing with me—and one time succeeding and feeling for the first time, with a bit of shock, the little sandpaper tongue lick my hand. My mother did not care for cats, thinking them "sneaky," but what I always remember accompanying her disdain for the creatures was an emphatic statement that she would never harm one, nor stand by idly while someone else harmed one. Her position on cats gradually transformed into a core value for me—just because I didn't care for some group or some individual was not a reason to harm them or condone others harming them. My mother wisely took the lesson one step further by declaring, "Dislike should never be a barrier to kindness."

My grandfather was laid to rest in the Thorsby cemetery just on the outskirts of town, where all of my departed Collins relatives are buried. I remember being placed in the care of my mother's baby sister, Aunt Gail, during the funeral. I remember her dabbing at her eyes with a tissue, sad for my father's family loss, and trying her best to answer the questions that I kept asking about death and heaven and what happens next.

When purchased in 1958, the big house featured an outdoor bathroom, known as an outhouse. My mother told a hilarious story about her and my father spending the night in the big house a year or so before I was born. The story goes that my father got up in the night to use the privy and in the process accidentally sat down on a hen roosting in the outhouse. When the soft feathers touched his bare bottom, accompanied by the low cooing of the disturbed hen, my father apparently bolted from the outhouse with the fear of the damned. His flight, hampered and hobbled by his drawers down around both ankles, was trailed by a string of colorful verbs and adverbs that hung suspended for an instant in the damp night air. My mother, who apparently was waiting her turn and was eye witness to the entire scene, lost her breath laughing.

After my grandfather's death in 1968, my grandmother, with one child remaining at home, was soon rattling around in the big house. Once again the eldest children pooled their resources and bought her a small two-bedroom house on the corner of Iowa and Jefferson, just a few blocks away. "The little house" is the fixture of my teenaged memories and where I stayed on weekend respites from the duplex. I loved spending time with my grandmother in that little house. It featured the requisite front porch swing with chains that creaked melodiously as it swung and a closed-in back porch that housed the most wonderful bed I have ever slept on. The mattress was glorious, albeit only for a teenager's back. Once I had sat on the side, I was naturally rolled to the middle, where both halves would then fold toward each other, making me feel safe and warm and somewhat like a human taco. Later in the night, the train would predictably pass through town, sounding its whistle, signaling order and routine, and I would sleep, deep and dreaming. The kitchen was also a magical place as my grandmother was a gifted cook. She had this silver tablespoon that had whipped up so many recipes over the years that it was actually flattened on its top left side, indicative of her right-handed mixing motions. On occasion, she would bake her famous pecan pie, and the entire house would fill with the mouth-watering aroma. Be it pie, homemade biscuits, leftover cornbread, or the remnants of a pot of black-eyed peas, there was always something delightful to snack on, either resting atop the white enamel stove or in a tin-foil covered plate sitting on the Formica table.

If my mother's relationship with her mother was mysterious to me, my father's relationship with his mother was confounding. Being born in the middle of the ten, my father exhibited some of the classic behaviors ascribed to the middle child. He was an attention seeker, even if it meant he had to act out to get it; and it seemed to me that he always wanted more from his mother than she was able to give—more attention, more favor, more love. When her behavior was deemed unacceptable to him, he would become angry, sometimes sulky. After my grandfather's death, she and my teenaged uncle Royce visited us in Titusville. I remember my father reprimanding my grandmother when he observed her staring longingly out the sliding glass doors of our house as she had shyly told him she missed home, which he had taken as an insult. On one occasion at the big house after my grandfather's passing, my father became so upset with her that he actually put her over his knee and spanked her like a child. I was horrified and quickly left the room in an attempt to relieve at least a modicum of embarrassment for my grandmother. There were other family members in the house at the time; and I remember returning, when I believed the coast to be clear, only to feel the unease that had fallen over the entire house, all of us trying to make sense of my father's breach of family mores.

My mother seemed to enjoy spending time with her mother-in-law and seemed to have an engrained soft spot for her. I believe she viewed my grandmother's life as having been mostly work with very little play and sought to introduce her to different experiences. Within a few years after my grandfather's death, however, my grandmother began to exhibit signs of what everyone identified back then as "hardening of the arteries." As her behavior became less and less predictable, the family naturally feared for her safety and decided to house her in a facility designed to care for adults with significant functional and memory loss. My grandmother went on to "live" under the ravaging affects of what we now realize was Alzheimer's disease until she succumbed to pneumonia on August 9, 1986. Her children paid regular visits over the years, but when my grandmother eventually forgot who my father was, that added the final insult to his injury.

Our return to Alabama allowed all three of us to spend quality time with members of my father's family with whom we had special relationships. My dad spent many of his pre-employment hours with his older brother, W. A., number two in the line-up. Uncle W. A., aside from being a great father and husband and the de facto patriarch of the Collins clan, was a gifted mechanic and a natural engineer. He leased a building on the south side of Thorsby and operated a garage out of it. The "W. A. (Bill) Collins Garage" was indeed a place of wonder. It was huge, filled with tools and lifts and grease-stained workbenches, and served as a haven for my father. Just inside and to the right of the large garage door, stood a short Coke machine that still delivered the little 6 1/2 ounce, ice-cold Coca-Colas in the green glass bottle for a dime. Close by was a big Tom's Jar with a screw on lid full of little cracker sandwiches of peanut butter or cheese. A small square office space sat behind the Coke machine. It contained an old desk, cluttered with greasy fingerprint stained bills and receipts, and featured an antique wooden swivel chair that creaked with anyone's weight and always seemed to sit its occupant a little cattywampus. Along with memories of my father and my uncle in this mechanic's wonderland, I also have vivid mental pictures of the two of them—so similar in looks and mannerisms as to have easily passed for twins instead of brothers eight years apart—sitting on my uncle's little glassed-in porch, just off his kitchen, smoking cigarettes, drinking coffee, arguing football, and solving the problems of the world.

My mother also had a soft spot for my aunt Helen, number four in the line-up, and the uncontested black sheep of the Collins clan. Aunt

Helen had made some interesting choices when it came to partners, and those partners had not always had her best interests at heart. I remember a specific visit my mother and I made to Aunt Helen's house, just a few yards down from the big house. The three of us gathered in the kitchen, and while my aunt busied herself with this and that, I took a seat at the table and listened politely to their conversation. Aunt Helen was a very hard worker and had a superb sense of humor, but on this day, knowing my mother was both ally and friend, she was lamenting some of the recent events in her life. As she scrubbed the top of her white enamel stove to a lusty shine, she made the statement, "Kathryn, things could not be any worse." My wise mother replied, "Helen, things can always be worse." My aunt smiled and chuckled a little, I suppose realizing my mother was right.

One of Aunt Helen's children, my cousin Gary, was singled out by my mother for some extra attention, I believe because she thought he could use it. Cousin Gary, with his dominant Collins blond hair and blue eyes, was two years younger than I and was one of my favorite cousins. My mother loved him equally as much as I did. Gary spent the entire summer of 1971 with us in Titusville, and we had a splendid time together. Clearest in my memory was the morning we rose at 3 a.m. in order to get to the Central Florida Farmer's Market in time to set up the carrots he and I had harvested the day before and wished to sell. My mother's dear friend, D., and her husband farmed ten or so acres several miles inland from Titusville; and on this particular weekend my mother had agreed for the three of us to help her with the gathering, the washing, and finally the selling of the vegetables the following day. As Ms. D. laid out the plan, Gary and I thought nothing of the scheduled 4 a.m. departure—until the next morning at 3 a.m. when we tried to pry our eyes open. Although by that time in the summer carrots were actually on the decline, Ms. D. agreed that if Gary and I could harvest a bunch and make them presentable, we could keep any profit from their sale. As the morning wore on, our carrots were passed up by one buyer and then another. Finally, a representative from a chain of southern grocery stores stopped by our table and allowed the two eager youngsters to talk him into buying the sad looking carrots, the green tops now clearly wilted by the heat of the day. As the grocery store representative walked away with the fruits of our labor, Gary and I celebrated like gifted athletes, shuffling and jingling the coins in our pockets.

That summer sped by, and soon my mother began to lay plans for Gary's return to Alabama in time for the start of the school year. She and my father decided that Gary, Mom, and I would fly back to Birmingham. Dad would drive up a few days later and take Gary back to Thorsby. I think during that summer my mother may have been living out a small fantasy of having both a daughter and a son because she bought similar traveling outfits for Gary and me to wear on the plane, signaling to any passer-by that these two young people belonged to her.

In the ensuing years, Gary and I naturally drifted apart. We still loved each other dearly, but school and careers and families of our own soon sent us in opposite directions. In 1993 I received a telephone call from my father telling me that Gary had taken his own life. I remember being shocked as my mind began the fruitless search for an answer to the question "why?" My mother, I knew, would be deeply saddened by this news so I used her very example and was visibly empathetic and compassionately direct when I delivered it.

As an officer in the US Army, Gary was given a military funeral, and when the lone bugler, whom no one could see, began to play "Taps," I felt the tears sting my eyes and once again questioned if there was anything I could have done to stop it. The crack of rifle fire from the guns firing the 21-gun military salute, jolted me from my melancholy, and the words my dear mother often used came to me, "What's done is done, and cannot be undone."

My mother delighted in the musical talents of the Collins family, and particularly loved to hear my cousin Randall play the guitar and sing. Randall, Uncle W. A.'s only son, had a beautiful voice and cheerfully played "The Green, Green Grass of Home" every time my mother requested it—and she requested it every time we saw him. Randall was genuine and kind, but without the gruff exterior of my uncle (an exterior which was thin indeed as one had to scratch only a millimeter off the surface to find my uncle's true character). Randall and my uncle were cut from the same bolt of wonderful cloth. My mother commented more than once through the years that she wished my dad had been a little more like Uncle W. A.

The Collins family member that my mother adored was the second son of my aunt Bennie Gail, number seven in the line-up. My aunt married a man whose last name was also Collins; so she remained Bennie Gail Collins when she married Sammy Joe Collins in 1962. Their son Brandon was born in July 1974, and my uncle Sam actually stopped by our duplex to pick up my mother and carry her to the hospital with my very pregnant aunt so that he wouldn't have to be alone during the labor and delivery. My mom was literally there from the moment Brandon was born and began babysitting him almost immediately, as my aunt was slated to complete her practice teaching assignment at a local grammar school at the start of the school year.

As for me, our return to Alabama allowed me to spend some time under the loving wing of my cousin Lydia, youngest daughter of Uncle W. A. My lovely blond, green-eyed cousin was chronologically only six months older, but was light years ahead of me in every other respect. She was very gracious to me during those odd months and included me in her church youth group activities and other outings with her friends. Lydia had spent several weeks with us in Titusville one summer just a few years before we made our move back to Alabama. During that summer visit, she had ridden to my rescue by introducing me to the more modern accoutrement of feminine hygiene. Words cannot describe my gratitude to her for that. She had a wonderful personality and a gift with people, and I watched her like a hawk, absorbing and learning.

One day while I was visiting with Big Momma, sitting on the couch on the enclosed porch watching television, I heard my father call out to me as he came through the front door. I got up immediately and met him in the kitchen. With a grin that showed every tooth in his mouth, he pulled a yellow slip of paper from his pocket and showed it to me. It had the figure $600.00 written on it. That was the monthly offer he had received from the Goodyear Tire Company. My mouth dropped open at the size of it. Just as we suspected, offers for employment from various places had begun to materialize even though it had been only a few months since we had arrived from Florida. He decided to decline the offer from Goodyear and instead took an offer from Alabama Power Company, a vertically integrated electric utility that served most of the state of Alabama. He would, within five years of being hired by Alabama Power as an Engineering Aide I, become a construction supervisor. For the next several years he was assigned to one construction project after another across the state as the company increased its electric generating capacity by building coal-fired steam plants, hydro-electric dams, and a nuclear power plant.

With this new job securely in hand, my parents began in earnest to look for our next home; and in the late summer of 1974, they found a nice three-bedroom, two-bath ranch-style house situated on about three acres in the central Alabama countryside. It was quiet and comfortable, and my father began almost immediately making improvements. He built himself a large outbuilding for his mechanical piddling and then closed in our two car garage with a rock and mortar fireplace. He also built a small horse stable with an attached tack room for the beautiful dun horse my parents would soon gift me on my sixteenth birthday. Our house was on a dirt road that gave way to other dirt roads, a wonderful place to ride a horse. Although my mother had ridden horses many times during her vacations in Fontana, she was basically distrustful of them, perhaps recognizing that was a tremendous amount of power under the control of a brain the size of a walnut. Her trust in my beautiful horse was not increased as she watched me from the kitchen sink window one cold January morning as I was feeding him and saw him kick me on the inside of my left knee when I gently patted his rump while making my way around his rear-end to exit his pen. In my life to date, that kick remains the single most acutely painful thing I have ever felt. My mother said that tears sprang forthwith to her own eyes as she vicariously experienced the painful kick that had literally dropped me to my knees.

As was our custom, once settled in a new place, we began to look for a new church home. We visited a few, but settled on one within reasonable driving distance from our new house. My parents immediately began to involve themselves in the various activities of the church, my dad as a deacon and a tenor in the choir and my mom as a Sunday School teacher and Women's Missionary Union director. I was old enough now to join the adult choir and took my place amongst the altos. I enjoyed singing very much and occasionally would have the opportunity to sing a duet or a solo. My mother had some great advice for me when I began to sing songs outside of the choir that would cause the attention of the congregation to be focused entirely on me. She offered, "Don't fall in love with the attention you may receive from singing; remember, it is a gift and you are singing for Jesus, not for yourself." I have sung numerous times in church venues over the last four decades and have had to fight that ego that wants to celebrate and say, "Look what I have done." My weapon of choice in that fight is my mother's wisdom—my pre-performance prayer being, "Not I, not I, but the wind that blows through me."

My mother, as I had already witnessed in Florida, was very faithful in the execution of her duties, continuing to prepare thoroughly and well in advance to teach her Sunday School class and going the extra mile for the Women's Missionary Union by dressing the part of a typical female in the featured foreign country. She would also prepare ethnic recipes for the WMU members to sample, trying to lend a better understanding of the life of a missionary in that country. The year India was the country of study, Mom bought some colorful material and draped it over and around her body as best she could to illustrate a sari and taught the lesson dressed so. That WMU study of India also afforded me my first taste of chicken curry as that particular spice had never before been a feature in my mom's culinary repertoire. I also learned about the versatility of rice, a main side dish in the Indian diet, and found it a reasonable substitute for potatoes, which in the South were the preferred "eat with everything" vegetable.

Many small churches in the South are replete with intricate family ties that are not obvious on the surface. Our new church home was no different. Layers of cousins, deep into the third and fourth strata, abounded in the small church, and my mother made me laugh when she teased that one had best not speak ill of anyone in our congregation because assuredly the malicious words would either be spoken directly to an unrealized relative or overheard by one.

I learned a great deal from watching my mother interact with members of our new church. In total, the learning was to do my own thinking. She taught me that I would always encounter people during my life more than willing to hand me their own pre-packaged opinions and conclusions, but that it was incumbent upon me to think through the situation for myself and do my own critical analysis. If after thoughtful reflection, I came to the same opinion or same conclusion, that was fine; but it was important that I come to it under my own steam.

She exemplified this important teaching when she herself spoke the lone "No" against a particular candidate for deaconship during a customary voice vote one Sunday evening. This candidate had divorced his first wife years earlier and was now happily remarried with children. But my mother believed that the qualifications for pastors and deacons given in 1 Timothy 3 was the guidance that should be used when a church congregation chose a pastor or deacons. Verse twelve, in almost all translations, states that deacons should have only one wife. My mother's prayerfully considered opinion was that divorced men did not meet that qualification and therefore this man was not a viable candidate. He perhaps was the only person not surprised by my mother's rejection, however, because she had gone to him many days prior to the vote and told him that she had prayed for guidance and believed that the Scripture was clear and because of his divorce he was not eligible for deaconship; she added that she believed him to be a fine young man, with a lot to offer the church in other capacities, but had to vote both her conscience and her convictions. He told my mother that he understood and thanked her for being honest with him in advance. I was in the congregation during that voice vote and although my opinion of the Scripture's meaning differed from my mother's, I was nonetheless very proud of her for being strong enough to stand firm on what she believed. I was also very impressed with the respect she had afforded the young man prior to the vote.

Shortly after we became members, my mother, along with a few other church members, was made part of a pastor search committee. The committee was diligent and often traveled to other cities, sometimes in other states, to hear a prospective pastor preach. They finally reached a decision and invited a man, whom I will call Lawrence Riley, for a trial sermon; and after a successful first-go, the committee made him an offer which he accepted. Brother Riley had been called to preach later in life and, along with an impressive set of academic credentials, had a most interesting past, including a time when he himself was both a ruffian and an unbeliever. My mother was circumspect about the Rileys, hoping that she and the other committee members had not been too impressed by his pedigree to render a balanced judgment on his pastoring skills.

Brother Riley was married to an interesting lady, whom I will give the name Lisa. Lisa was several years his junior, and together they had a young son. Among Lisa's oddities, at least to me, was the fact that she did not believe it was appropriate to have a television in their home and did not permit her son to watch it at all. She did not judge others for having a television, however. My father, always looking for comic material, noted that whenever Lisa visited our house, which usually had the television playing softly in the background, she would struggle mightily to keep her focus on the conversation, her head turning routinely to take in the moving picture playing off to her side. My mother thought her unique also but refused to judge her, saying simply that she marched to a different drummer.

If he was anything, Brother Riley was both creative and theatrical. For every sermon, he would give our organist and our pianist a key word or a phrase to remember, and when he spoke it, that was their signal to rise from the front pew, retake their seats at the organ and the piano, and begin softly playing the invitational hymn. He might use "Marilyn Monroe" or "yesterday's news" or some other catchy phrase worked brilliantly into his closing remarks to signal the musicians.

I recall one absolutely unforgettable sermon on Exodus 32 during which he produced a gold spray-painted ceramic bull from behind the lectern and set it atop the pulpit. It was completely visible to the congregation and symbolic of the actions of Aaron and the Israelites, recorded in verses two, three and four, whilst Moses was atop Mt. Sinai visiting with the Lord and obtaining the two tablets of covenant law. Brother Riley continued the sermon by telling how the Lord knew immediately that the Israelites under Aaron's leadership had become corrupt and that He was basically fed up with them. Moses, totally ignorant of their current shenanigans, came running to their rescue, pleading and arguing his case on behalf of the Israelites. The Bible records that his arguments prevailed and "the Lord relented." As Moses returned from the mountain with the Ten Commandments in hand, he heard singing from the camp. As he approached, he saw the golden calf they had produced and were worshipping and verse nineteen records, "He burned with anger." At this point in his sermon, approaching the crescendo, Brother Riley replicated Moses' anger with his own voice, made an empty handed motion with his arms to illustrate Moses dropping the tablets, and then lifted the gold-painted ceramic bull high above his head and threw it to the carpeted floor, shattering it into dozens of pieces. The entire congregation jumped with a collective sharp intake of breath; and for a second, we all feared for the cardiac health of those precious senior citizens who always sat near the front and typically nodded off about halfway through the sermon. When we got back home, my parents and I giggled all the way through the delicious Sunday dinner Mother had prepared, featuring the fried wafer-thin pork chops that my father loved, asking each other between bites, "Did you see ole' so-and-so jump when Brother Riley dropped that bull?"

The Rileys stayed at our church for only a few years, and upon their departure the committee was back at work looking for the next shepherd. This time the selection was a fellow whom I will call David Marlowe. Brother David did not have the same educational background as Brother Riley but perhaps was more relatable to the middle-class Southerners who made up the bulk of our membership. He did have the formal Bible training necessary to lead the congregation and was the pastor for the next few decades. His wife was a delightful woman, with an easy laugh and a great personality, and she and my mother developed a very good and long lasting friendship.

This church was to be the backdrop for several significant events in my mother's life, and in this church she would meet two exceptional friends who would help her navigate the rough waters that were destined to come her way, including the empty nest I would soon leave behind and my father's betrayal.

The first of the two friends, several years my mother's junior, was a lovely lady named Jennifer. A few years after the move to our country home, Jennifer and her husband, Thomas, purchased several acres of land adjoining ours. They planted fruit trees on much of the property; and on a lovely spot under some mature hardwoods toward the middle of their acreage, they began the construction of their home. Thomas was a talented carpenter and like my father could do almost anything. Prior to their ownership, the property directly behind us was generally unkempt and had a bit of a neglected look, which likely contributed to my father unwittingly constructing one corner of my horse barn about three yards across our actual back property line. I think my father hoped the new owners wouldn't notice, but that was not my mother's way. Jennifer remembers my mother being the first person to introduce herself to them on the Sunday morning of their initial visit to our church; and soon after the introduction, my mother told them of our unintentional mistake. Jennifer and her husband were very gracious and allowed the barn to stay where it was originally constructed.

Despite their age difference, Jennifer and my mother became the closest of friends. They had the type of friendship that, by my estimation, comes along only once or twice in a lifetime: the kind of relationship where each could pour her heart out, tell of her innermost thoughts and know it would go no further. They would freely and routinely just show up unannounced at each other's house for a visit without a second thought. There was absolutely no pretense between them, each allowing the other to be totally herself. They even enjoyed doing ordinary things together like canning—forming an assembly line, each with a specific task, as they prepared the vegetables that Thomas and Jennifer had either grown themselves or bought. My mother also cared deeply for Thomas and their children, occasionally babysitting their youngest while Jennifer attended to some obligation. Mom and Jennifer shared the intricacies of their lives in measure with the love, mutual respect, and trust they had for each other. During the difficult years surrounding my parents' divorce, I was obligated to a career in another city several hours away and was supremely grateful that Jennifer was so close by.

The second friend, Ms. Ellen, was my mother's contemporary and running buddy. If Mom caught a wild hare, then Ms. Ellen would get a call. I met her many times and could easily see why my mother loved her. She was kind and gracious and loads of fun. Ms. Ellen was married to a very sweet gentleman named Theodore; and even when Mr. Theo became confined to his wheelchair, Mom and Ms. Ellen wouldn't hesitate to load him up and drive to the casinos in Philadelphia, Mississippi, to play the one-armed bandits, putting a self-disciplinary limit on the amount they would bet, lest it be judged as full blown "gamblin'." In the summers of the early to mid-1990s, Ms. Ellen, Mr. Theo, and Jennifer would come to Mom's house several times a week for lunch and a few hours of Rook. Ms. Ellen was a card player extraordinaire, and of the other three, whoever was paired with her usually took the victory lap. When Ms. Ellen passed away in the late 1990s, she was only seventy-four, and my mother was deeply saddened by the loss. In the subsequent years, I would need all my fingers and toes to count the number of times I heard my mother say, "I sure do miss Ellen."

The move from the duplex to our country home signaled yet another change of schools for me; so in September 1974 I was enrolled in a different high school in the county. I was very fortunate to fall in with a group of good young people who were fun and yet serious about their studies, among them my dearest friend, Erin. I was also blessed to have a gifted mathematics teacher at this school, and that instructor stands as the most gifted instructor I have ever had. Under that tutelage I fell in love with mathematics, which was foundational for my chosen field of study in college. Erin was, and still is, a genteel, kind soul whom I trust implicitly, and both of my parents loved her and were extremely happy that she and I had become best friends. My mother was keenly aware of the importance of "running with good people," telling me on more than one occasion how her own father had coached her by saying, "If you can't run with people as good as you, then run with people who are better."

Over the next three years, as I completed my sophomore, junior, and senior years of high school, my relationship with my mother was nothing short of smooth sailing, with only an occasional small wave to navigate over. In fact, it seemed that the typical head-on collisions between mothers and pubescent daughters were never a feature of our relationship. I can account for that only by giving total credit to my mother's wisdom. She knew there was an inevitable tipping point, fast approaching, where her role as manager, handling every detail of my life, would need to shift to that of trusted counselor. She was "letting out the rope" slowly and carefully, nosing the baby bird gently toward the edge of the nest. As for me, I was totally oblivious of these behind the scenes machinations and simply grew to trust her more than ever, never feeling the need to pull for my independence but rather sensing that it was being handed to me in carefully measured increments.

One particular thing that had always been good between us and never changed was our ability to play together. Several mornings a week, hours before classes started, we would drive to the courts and play a couple of sets of tennis. At first, I absolutely could not hang with her and she beat me routinely. But just as she had promised, over time my skill level increased and with my natural athleticism—a genetic gift from her—I began to win my share of games and then soon totally dominated our competitions. Ever graceful, my mother had always predicted that the novice would eventually become better than the coach.

The summer before my junior year in high school, I met the man I would eventually marry. I was playing first base for my traveling softball team in a small tournament in his hometown. He had recently graduated from college and was returning to the area to take his first job. On this particular afternoon, he had just happened to stop by to watch the ladies play softball and, as the story goes, after meeting me, went home and told his parents he had met his future wife. I was only sixteen when we met, just able to date; but he courted me for the next four years, and after I completed my sophomore year in college we were married.

My mother liked him, but, as I would learn years later, did not believe he was the right guy for me. She sensed his tendency to be possessive, never cruel, but certainly possessive and my mother feared I was too submissive by nature to stand my ground should it ever come down to that. She also saw the five-year age difference as a losing proposition for me. I had my final years of high school and college to think about whereas he was ready to settle down, already having sown his wild oats, so to speak. She worried that a serious relationship would interfere with me completing my studies and that troubled her a great deal. But, knowing human nature to be what it is, my mother feared that if she put her foot down against him that would only drive me toward him. So she stayed in counselor role for the most part—except for the afternoon I announced that I would work a year after high school before enrolling in college. On that note, she reverted back to manager and simply said, "No, if you do that you will never go to college." I have thanked her, silently and out loud, a million times over the years for that intervention.

Erin and I graduated from high school in 1977 and were Valedictorian and Salutatorian, respectively, of our Senior Class. I had received a partial scholarship to play basketball at a small liberal arts college in southwestern Alabama about an hour away from my home, and Erin had chosen to attend college an hour away in the opposite direction. Another of our friends, CelieAnn, was slated to be my roommate; but at the last minute for personal reasons, her plans changed. I remember my first dorm room—small, dimly lit, painted emergency-room green, with one tiny window that even I, standing five feet nine inches tall, couldn't see out of. I was very unhappy and missed my mother like a fish misses water. No matter how hard I tried, I could not stop crying. I wore contact lenses back then and completely ruined a pair because of all the salt deposits that had collected on the surface during those first few weeks of tearful orientation.

Inside the administration building, a long-distance telephone line was made available free to the students for fifteen-minute intervals and accessible according to a sign-up sheet. I made sure my name was on the list each and every evening after classes and always used my fifteen minutes to call my mother. At the sound of her voice, my own voice would break and despite my best efforts to have a tearless conversation with her, I would fail. Very similar to the talks we would have on the way to kindergarten thirteen years earlier, she encouraged me and gently assured me and loved me. She advised me, "Give it just a few more weeks, baby," and by so doing was masterfully cutting this huge challenge into bite-sized pieces that I could handle. I had never been away from her, never. I had not gone to camp; I had not spent a summer with a relative; I had always been close to her. But just as she had predicted, slowly but surely, I made the adjustment and began to make new friends, enjoy my studies, and engage in practice for the upcoming basketball season. It didn't hurt that my dormitory assignment got changed and brought with it a more modern room with large windows and best of all a precious, precious roommate. It also didn't hurt that I could easily drive home on Friday afternoon, and return to the campus Sunday afternoon.

Years later, my mother shared with me that the most difficult thing for her to do during those first two weeks of my college experience was to NOT get into the car and go rescue her baby girl. She fought down that powerful urge, knowing it was the wrong thing for her to do and realizing that it would definitely not be in my long-term best interest—I remain forever grateful.

At the end of my freshman year in May 1978, I decided to transfer to the University of Alabama at Birmingham to pursue a degree in Mass Communications. I think my parents always assumed I would become a veterinarian. I loved animals and had always had a dog. When I brought my hamster Peppi back from the dead when I was in the sixth grade, I think that clinched it for them. My parents told that story to anyone who would listen, and in my father's southern vernacular, it went something like this—"Cheri found that dang thang dead as a hammer layin' in the bottom of its cage. She got it out, laid it on its back, and put pancake syrup down its throat with an eye dropper. Then she did little one finger chest compressions for a minute or so, and that damn rat came back to life!" I honestly have no idea of the hamster physiology at work during that resurrection, but he did live for another three months and it did make a great story that my masterful story-telling father loved to embellish and share.

My mother's baby sister, Aunt Gail, offered me domicile in the finished basement of her and my uncle's large suburban home in Hoover, just a few miles from the UAB campus. I actually moved in early, at the beginning of the summer so that I could accept the job as a "girl Friday" in the Employment Office of Alabama Power Company in downtown Birmingham. That summer job allowed me to see with my own eyes what the job market really looked like. I saw prospective applicants with extremely impressive résumés in History or Sociology or Business come and then go, the vast majority of them never hearing back from us. But let an engineer come through the door, and a giant imaginary shepherd's crook would snake down the hall and whisk them away for an interview. It didn't seem to matter what they looked like either; their glasses might be held together with duct tape, or their pants pulled up almost under their armpits, but if they held an engineering degree, by golly, the power company was interested. None of this was lost on me;

and during my lunch hour one day I walked the thirteen blocks to the UAB campus and enrolled in the School of Engineering.

My grandmother Lucy also lived in the furnished basement of my aunt and uncle's home. She and my aunt had always lived together, as my aunt was only eleven when my grandfather passed away; and when Aunt Gail married Uncle Gary in 1958, he gladly accepted her as a permanent resident in their home. During that year of being roommates, so to speak, my relationship with my grandmother, which was already good, flourished. That year I saw up close and personal where my mother's spirit of adventure and fun had likely come from—her own mother. Occasionally, my grandmother and I would go on wonderful escapades; my favorite—accomplices slipping out of the house late at night and going for ice cream, taking care not to make any noise, even holding the car doors partially ajar with one hand until we had completely backed out of the driveway—like anybody in the house would have cared. The silent escape was thrilling, however, for both of us—and of course, the ice cream was wickedly delicious.

My grandmother also adhered to the Christian faith, and often times we would lie in her bed before bedtime and memorize Scriptures together. Our favorite was Romans 8: 38-39, and we worked hard to get our *angels and principalities*, and our *height* and our *depth* and our *things hoped for* and our *things to come* in the right order, finally deciding that it didn't really matter. We knew the part that mattered—*nothing could separate us from the love of God which is in Jesus Christ our Lord*. When the clock neared 7 p.m., I knew it was time for me to go into my quarters and allow her to listen to her favorite Christian broadcast on the radio. Bidding my grandmother goodnight reminded me of bidding my mother goodnight, the same sweet "I love you" given and returned.

I already knew my grandmother Lucy had a heroic streak in her after hearing the story of the surprise picnic rescue that she performed on my mother's behalf; but she had also performed a rescue for me, four years prior to us becoming roommates in my aunt's basement. My parents were out of town, and although I was fifteen years old and capable of staying by myself, I couldn't legally drive. My grandmother was providing me transportation hither and yon and staying in the house with me. My little dog, Tiny, half Chihuahua and half Toy Manchester

Terrier, had accompanied us from Florida. That particular morning she had been exploring her new surroundings when she apparently crossed into the territory of an aggressive neighborhood dog who literally tore her up. My grandmother, who was not an animal person, realized something was terribly wrong when she saw Tiny trudging home down our dirt road with an odd bulge under her abdomen, apparently propelled forward by her instinct for survival. My grandmother swung into action. She managed to get Tiny into her little straw bed, put her in the car, and then drove to the high school to get me. She went inside the principal's office, explained what was going on, and had them page me. I couldn't imagine why I was being paged to come to the principal's office but quickly figured out that something wasn't right when I saw my grandmother. I jumped into the front seat and peered into the back and saw Tiny's little brown eyes starring straight ahead, at nothing; I learned later she was in shock. We drove to the veterinarian's office. He announced he couldn't take any actions to address her wounds until she came out of shock; so he put her on a heating pad, made her comfortable, and we waited. Tiny survived that close call and her survival was due totally to my grandmother—to her quick thinking, her quick action, and her ability to put her love for me above her reluctance to be around dogs.

In August 1979 with a total of two years of college under my belt, with one of those being a year of engineering school, I married. My husband and I moved into a nice brick home, located a dozen or so miles from my parents' home. Much to my parents' delight, after marrying I continued my classes at UAB, making the long commute. For the next two years I scheduled classes straight through the summers and graduated in December 1981.

I took an entire weekend off before starting my first job, which was with Southern Natural Gas Company as a project engineer—oddly enough, the same company my father worked for sixteen years earlier when he dropped the little gray parachute into our backyard with that stocking full of Christmas goodies. My husband and I never went hungry during our first two years of marriage, but the budget was very, very tight. We couldn't wait to add an additional paycheck and give ourselves a little financial breathing room.

During my last two years of college, which were also my first two years of marriage, I remained as close to my parents as was reasonable for someone who seemed to always be studying for an exam and was now married and living in a different household. My husband and I visited with them, had dinner with them fairly often, and also attended church services with them. I remember my relationship with my mother taking on a different cast during the early years of my marriage, nothing strained or awkward: she just treated me like the married woman that I was. She was very circumspect about the potential success of my marriage but kept those thoughts to herself, aside from sharing them with her precious friend Jennifer, which was the equivalent of keeping them to herself. She was determined to be a supportive mother-in-law, pretty much keeping her distance, allowing us to forge our own marital path. My husband admired my mother a great deal and appreciated her approach, even when she privately warned him that he needed to get a handle on his possessiveness, lest I grow to resent it one day. Although none of us knew it then, my mother's prediction of rough winds ahead would come to pass; but for the time being at least, I was content.

My grandparents and my mom

Mom's high school senior picture

Mom studying her school lessons

Mom with her high school sweetheart, N.
—the guy with the long eyelashes

Mom, back row, far right, with her high school basketball team

Mom looking pretty, chin resting
in one of those beautiful hands

Mom, age 23, posing on a boat

Mom enjoying a sandwich and a Coke

Mom with friends at the telephone company
in Birmingham, December, 1951

Mom, Aunt Millie, and a friend, showing off their legs

Mom and Aunt Wilma as friends on the beach—
before they became sisters-in-law

Mom and one of the many young people she took under her wing

Mom with her niece, Lynn

Mom in nurses training, age 21

Mom and Dad, March 5, 1955

Mom in Texas with a stringer of fish

Mom and Dad on vacation in Canada, June 1956

Mom, pregnant with me in Texas. She wrote on the back of this photo, "I look like a Jersey cow—but it's hard to sit with a big tummy and big boots, too. HA!" August, 1958

Dad, Mom and me at six months old

Aunt Gail and Uncle Gary in Miami, Florida, 1969

Dad working on a plane at Southern Natural Gas
Company, Birmingham, Alabama

Me, Tiny and Dad at the beach in Titusville, Florida

Mom looking pretty and thin
—Christmas at Aunt Gail's house

Mom's all-time favorite photo of me and
my dad—Fontana, North Carolina

Mom and Dad dressed up for church in Titusville, Florida

Mom developed a green thumb in Titusville

Dad in the red dune buggy

Mom jumping the dune!

Mom and friends, filthy, following an afternoon of
trailing Dad and me in our dune buggy

Mom and Eeyore, Walt Disney World, Orlando, Florida

Dad with all nine of his siblings, various cousins, and in-laws and Lady, the German Shepherd, 1987

Mom on the deck at my lake home, Eufaula, Alabama, just weeks before her passing

May 10, 1998

Hi Sweetness,

I'm ready a little early for SS. and I'm dropping you a line —

I'm sending you a picture of me, which I don't like because it looks just like me —

I'm like Roy Rogers. He ~~and~~ says everytime he smiles his eyes disappear.

Going to Bham after SS. Lynn wanted to include me on her mother's day lunch with her mom & dad. I love you darling

Mom

A letter from Mom displaying her characteristic sense of humor

4

I f it had been medically advisable for my mother, I think my parents would have enjoyed having more children. She was thirty-two years old while pregnant with me and I was her third and only full-term pregnancy. In September 1958, although she was five months along, her doctor strongly advised against the eleven-hour road trip from Copperas Cove, Texas, to Birmingham, Alabama, to attend her baby sister's wedding. When she mildly protested his advice, he simply asked her, "Do you want to see your sister get married or have a healthy baby?" Mom said the answer to that question was easy and chose to stay put.

My mother was one of those women naturally steeped in maternal instinct and had feathered her nest early for any baby bird that might need to take refuge there. From the age of her accountability well into her seventies, my mother had an assortment of young people in her life, who without question benefited from that association. Before she married, she was prone to take unrelated youngsters under her wing and just expose them to fun things, and of course her loving self. One such youngster was a boy whom I will call Tommy Johnson. Tommy was being raised by his grandparents in the small town of Thomas, Alabama, just two miles northeast of Birmingham. My grandmother, my mother, and my aunt Gail had moved to Thomas shortly after my grandfather's death in March 1949. I am certain my mother saw in Tommy a child who could use a little extra love and attention; therefore she jumped at the opportunity to play the role of big sister, spending time with him, taking him places he would otherwise not be able to go, and certainly protecting him, if necessary.

Some of Mom's assortment of young people were her nieces and nephews, and I am certain if she were alive today she would emphatically state she loved all of them equally. But, there were a few relationships that were unique and special. On the Collins side of the family, there was Brandon, whom my mother fell in love with practically from the moment he drew his first breath; and on the Adams side, two nieces and a nephew held special places in my mother's heart.

Lynn, Aunt Millie and Uncle Ralph's daughter, was the first child born to any of my mother's siblings. She was born in 1953, before my mother married, and their relationship was extremely special and remained so throughout my mother's life. Marygail was born in March 1966, and because Aunt Millie and her family lived in Pensacola she was able to keep that pregnancy a complete secret. When the family showed up at Aunt Millie's home for Easter holidays that year, she walked out to greet us with this baby in her arms. It was love at first sight for Mom. Throughout Marygail's pre-school years, her parents allowed her to visit us often. She was the delight of the Adams clan and the baby of the entire Adams family for the next six years.

In April 1972 we all gathered in the living room of Aunt Gail and Uncle Gary's home in Hoover and waited anxiously for the arrival of the little boy whom we knew was going to be carried through that front door at any moment. My aunt and uncle had adopted a newborn baby boy after years of unsuccessful attempts to have a biological child of their own. They named him Gavin. When my mother saw him in the arms of her beloved baby sister, she melted. Just like Lynn, Marygail, and Brandon, Gavin settled into a corner of my mother's heart and never left.

Because her affection was universal, some of her special young people were the sons, daughters and grandchildren of her friends. In that category, there was Robbie from Titusville and Jay, youngest son of Ms. Nita and Mr. Eugene, my parents' best friends from their Texas Army days. Jay was born in 1968, and since we visited the Phillips family at their Dadeville, Alabama, home regularly through the 1970s, my mother was able to be a part of his young life. Jay was a gifted athlete, right up my mother's alley. Beginning when he was a youngster and continuing into his teenaged years, my mother and Jay played a lot of golf together, and played at some lovely and quite expensive courses, courtesy of Ms. Nita. My favorite Mom/Jay golf story is the one where Ms. Nita treated them to eighteen holes at the lovely Lake View course at Callaway Gardens in Pine Mountain, Georgia. Ms. Nita was driving a big Cadillac in those days and gave Mom the keys so she could drive herself and Jay to the course. Mom recounted that she and Jay felt like total "fat cats," driving the Cadillac to the club drop off area and later signing in at the club house as if they owned the place. They got tickled, however, when Jay took off his tennis shoes to put on his golf shoes and displayed a gigantic hole in the bottom of one sock, realizing their "fat cat" facade had just been exposed.

When I married in 1979, knowing how much my mother loved babies, I expected that within a few years she would begin hinting for a grandchild, but she never did. My husband and I had actually planned to try to start a family at about the seven-year mark in our marriage. We reasoned that would be enough time for me to finish my degree and be far enough along into a career as to be eligible for maternity leave. Children never became a reality for me; so therefore grandchildren never became a reality for my mother. For all of my life, I had tried very hard never to disappoint her; and if no grandchildren of her own was indeed a disappointment, she never let me know it.

Not being the type of person to sit around twiddling her thumbs, Mom understandably looked for new challenges and new ways to occupy her time after I moved out of the house. She made application with the U.S. Postal Service but soon discovered that those jobs were indeed few and far between and very difficult to come by. She and I agreed years later that the axiom she believed in so strongly, "Everything happens for a reason," had been in play when the U.S. Postal Service job never came to fruition. I, for one, couldn't imagine that delivering mail on a rural route where she seldom came into contact with people would satisfy her inner nurturing self.

In 1979 she applied for a position as an aide on a school bus that transported mentally and physically challenged students; in 1983, not yet having obtained an aide's job, she submitted another application for bus driver, putting her name in the hat so to speak, queuing up for the next open spot that would one day materialize. When she discussed her plans with me, I encouraged her and thought it a wonderful idea; I knew she was a very good driver, she loved little people, and she was as compassionate a person as I had ever known—it was a triad of skills that seemed perfectly matched to her new pursuit.

The months from August 1979 (when I married) to July 1982 seemed peaceful and ordinary. I had finally finished my degree and was working at my first job. My mother was busying herself with her various church-related responsibilities, taking care of my dad, and occasionally taking short vacations with her sisters and her friends. Dad was systematically progressing to jobs with increasing responsibility within the power company. As a construction foreman, he did a fair amount of work away from home, sometimes for several months at a time, but would typically travel home for the weekends. We all continued to attend church together and contribute in our own unique ways; and my parents seemed to be content with each other. It was, however, as the saying goes, the calm before the storm.

In March 1982 my husband applied for and got his dream job. Knowing this was a job he had always wanted, I encouraged him to take it, and I began almost immediately to look for an engineering position in the same part of the state.

During my job search I moved back into my parents' home and commuted Monday through Friday to work at Southern Natural Gas Company in Birmingham; then to south Alabama each Friday afternoon to spend the weekend with my husband; and then back to my parents' home on Sunday to ready myself for the next week of work. It was not hard at all living with my parents again, especially with my mother.

It took me three months to find a job near my husband's new place of employment. In July 1982 I was offered and accepted a Jr. Engineer position at the Joseph M. Farley Nuclear Power Plant, owned and operated at that time by Alabama Power Company. In truth, I had no clue as to how a nuclear power plant worked, and I took the job because it was the only one I could find. My mother's belief that everything happened for a reason was once again prophetic, however, as I soon became fascinated with nuclear energy and spent the next thirty-one years working in various capacities in that field, retiring from Southern Nuclear Operating Company in 2014. For the second time, I had unwittingly followed in my father's professional footsteps, first with Southern Natural Gas Company and now with Alabama Power Company's nuclear power plant.

Construction on the two nuclear units had begun in 1970, and in 1975 my father was temporarily transferred to Dothan, Alabama, to lend his assistance as a construction foreman at the plant. Throughout his career with the power company, my father had built a stellar name for himself. His strong work ethic coupled with his wonderful personality and quick wit made him popular with co-workers and supervisors alike. Countless times over my thirty-one year career, someone would incidentally connect me with my father and without fail would comment most favorably about their experiences working with him. "Oh, you're Floyd Collins's daughter?" they would say. "I loved working with your father!" In response, I always found myself standing up a little taller, my chest swelling with pride.

During the few months my dad was working at the nuclear plant, my mother and I traveled to Dothan in the summer of 1975 to spend a few days with him. While Dad worked during the day, Mom and I would explore the area and do one of our favorite things, eat out. Dad had given us directions to a wonderful restaurant called Redmond's that specialized in fried shrimp just on the outskirts of Dothan. I remember our first drive to that restaurant providing the experience that formed the foundation for my belief in guardian angels.

I was sixteen years old and, of course, insisted on driving wherever Mom and I went. As we ventured toward Redmond's that afternoon on the narrow two-lane county road, a car proceeded to pass us on our left. Instead of using the full width of the on-coming lane to pass, he cut it very close and used a goodly portion of my lane. My reaction was to swerve quickly to the right to avoid being hit and then just as swiftly to swerve left to keep us from contacting obstructions in the right-of-way. As my mother and I breathed simultaneous sighs of relief in response to the close call, she complimented me on my driving. I thanked her but told her honestly I wasn't sure I had anything to do with it and that during the entire maneuver I had sensed an invisible force on the steering wheel, moving it underneath the grip of my hands. She commented without pause, "Oh, that was your guardian angel," cementing my own belief in the divine superheroes.

My mother taught me a lot about driving a car on the roadway. I had been driving for years in the woods in my father's homemade dune buggies, but handling an automobile on the road and learning to be considerate of other drivers was something she taught me.

When I obtained my learner's permit at age fifteen, she would ride shotgun and allow me to practice on some seldomly traveled paved roads near our home. I specifically remember during one of my training sessions approaching my first big curve. I was nervous about it, and although I was driving rather slowly, I wasn't sure how I should attack it. I asked my mother what I should do, and I will never forget her answer. She said, "Don't worry, honey, the curve will take care of itself." And, of course, that is exactly what happened.

I also had a tendency to stare at the road just a few yards in front of the car, but she taught me to "drive looking down the road" and anticipate what actions I might need to take. She taught me to move over for on-ramping cars and to move underneath the "left hand turn with caution" green light, and if I didn't get an eventual opening in the traffic, to actually make the turn when I was sure the approaching cars were stopping as their light turned yellow, then red. This allowed cars in the turn lane to actually make some progress and not get stuck in the line behind someone who would turn only when the oncoming traffic produced a sizable gap.

She taught me, if it could be done safely, to allow signaling cars to change lanes in front of me. She believed this was the best way to keep the traffic flowing and benefited everyone on the road. If someone changed lanes in front of her without signaling, however, they would most certainly get a horn blast and a new name.

She also taught me a fool-proof parallel parking strategy that I have been using and impressing folks with for years; I always deflect those compliments back to my mom.

My dad's driving advice was also very good; he instructed that applying the brakes in a situation was not always the best option; sometimes maneuvering and speeding up was the right thing to do.

My mother made it clear that the best thing a driver could do for themselves, their passengers, and everyone else on the road in their vicinity was to stay focused on the task at hand. Never was her advice more sage that when I found myself in Florida after accidentally turning right onto Highway 19 instead of left as intended following a quick stop at a store in Thomasville, Georgia. As I relayed the story to my mom, I further confessed that I didn't notice my error for twelve miles and only then when I saw "Welcome to the Sunshine State" at the state line.

After that confession, she came up with a little parting message that was very cute and actually, as intended, stuck with me. She would say, "Now pretend there is a little me standing on your hood saying, 'Honey, pay attention to what you're doing.' " The reigning mascot for my campaign to be an excellent driver has been the little miniature Mom standing on my hood, gently reminding me to always stay focused when behind the wheel.

I arrived in Dothan in early July 1982, just days ahead of the start of my new job. I moved into the small house in the heart of the city that my husband had found and rented when he had arrived three months earlier. The little house was very charming and comfortable; we stayed there for a few months before finding a cheaper house out in the county that was not nearly as nice but acceptable. It was centrally located for my husband's job and actually closer to the nuclear plant, shortening my drive to work.

The storm clouds surrounding my parents marriage that had been brewing just out of sight for the last few months were starting to gather and broke open, so to speak—for me at least—with a phone call from my father. I had been in my new position at the nuclear plant for roughly a week, my first day being July 19, 1982, and was nervous about the lengthy personal call I was engaged in. But the subject matter was quite important; so I continued to listen as he laid out a point by point case on the difficulties of living with my mother. I was unclear on the purpose of his call, especially the timing, wondering why we had to talk about this subject on this day and at my new office. I had lived in the house with them for eighteen years and I knew the challenges of living with both of them. I suggested that they seek counseling; then I suggested he just tell her how unhappy he was and address the issues. When none of these seemed acceptable to him, I finally suggested that if he was that unhappy then he should just tell her and leave. Why this option was not chosen by my father, I will never know.

Years later, after both of my parents had passed away, I learned that my father had made similar, even more nonsensical calls to Aunt Gail, my mother's baby sister, during July that year. She shared with me that his calls were frequent, were always made while she was at work, and made no sense. Finally, being a bit fed up with the mysterious conversations she flat out asked him if he had a girlfriend, as his statements were suggestive but not definitive. My aunt believed she had finally put two and two together, and with loving compassion she shared the details of the unusual conversations with my mother.

My mother had her own suspicions that something was awry and shared those with her dear friend Jennifer earlier that summer, as this was not the first time during their marriage that my father had paid extra attention to another woman and my mother recognized the signs. She took no immediate action, however; I can only speculate that she assumed and hoped this infatuation would go the route others had when my father had had some sort of attraction for other women over the years—that being nowhere.

In the late 1990s my mother and I were enjoying a trip down memory lane together by looking through old photos and viewing old home movies that she had recently had professionally transferred to video cassette. We were watching a movie from our early days in Birmingham circa early 1960s of a church picnic at a nearby swimming hole, when a young woman in a bathing suit lounging on a towel appeared on the black and white film, mouthing something indecipherable to the cameraman. The film continued to focus on her face for a few seconds and then traveled slowly down her outstretched body, made a u-turn at her feet, and traveled slowly back up her legs, her torso, and finally her face once again. I was transfixed by the lecherous aspect of the film, and asked my mother who in the world was shooting it—"Your father," she answered.

When my mother was in her seventies she told me the story of the late night phone call that rang through one evening in the early years of their marriage. She had already gone to bed, and my father had stayed up to watch television. My mother was awakened by the call and picked it up on the bedside phone after just one ring, fearing the reason behind the call as we all do when the phone rings so late at night. Apparently my father had picked it up simultaneously and my mother heard him say, "Hello?" and then heard a feminine voice respond alluringly, "Well, hello." Then my father told the caller to hold on for a moment. Seconds later, my father appeared in the open doorway of their bedroom and in the dim light saw my mother holding the receiver. She said he spun around on a dime, hurried back to the den, and hung up the phone. She also shared with me that while we lived in Titusville one of her friends had tipped her off to some unusual behavior my father was displaying around a married woman who lived on our block.

Once in the late 1970s, after my father had been working for the power company for a while, my mother's instincts were once again aroused. For some reason she suspected the woman this time to be my father's co-worker. Her response to these suspicions was to ask Jennifer to accompany her one day to take Dad his lunch. When my father came into the front office, my mother gave him the bagged lunch she had prepared and then kissed him as a wife kisses a husband, right in front of the office staff. Jennifer and I suspect that the other woman was thought by my mother to be an office assistant and that my mom was simply marking her territory.

My father's earlier dalliances would have certainly provided a vivid backdrop for what my mother was suspecting in the summer of 1982, but when she received the anonymous, mean-spirited letter that pointed fingers and named names, her suspicions were fueled and she was compelled to confront him. The last of the cat slithered out of the bag when an elderly member of the choir observed my father engaged in conduct unbecoming. This observation was followed by a request from senior church leadership for my father to tender his resignation as deacon. Apparently, my father had anticipated the senior leadership's response and had driven my mother to Ms. Nita's house to stay for a few weeks to save her some amount of embarrassment as news of the event spread like wildfire along the small town grapevine.

Upon hearing additional pieces of the story in a phone call from my mother and concluding that this was indeed the end of their marriage,

I drove back to be near her and give her my support. I found her stoic, and very, very sad.

A few days later I wrote a stinging rebuke to my father; although I no longer remember the details of the letter, I can easily recall the general theme. It went thus: I cannot believe you were such a coward. You were unwilling to take personal responsibility for your desire to be out of the marriage and instead tried to build a case against my mother to her friends, her family, and even me in order to justify your premeditated actions. I included a coup de grâce in the letter when I told him I didn't want to see him or speak to him.

Today, I deeply regret both the letter and the isolation, which, for the record, my mother did not support. She would always say, "He is your father and he loves you"; but I remained defiant. Almost three years would pass before I laid eyes on him or beloved members of my Collins family again; but in the words of the great Jane Austen, ". . . angry people are not always wise." During those three years, the vast majority of his comings and goings remained unknown to me—until I began writing this narrative. From the accounts of people with whom he sought refuge, including his siblings, he was melancholy and withdrawn, a completely altered state for my normal high-energy and jovial father. My father finally remarried in the late 1980s, several years after the divorce, in a private ceremony that few people, including me, knew anything about. I have reasoned over the years that my father was somewhat like the dog who loved to chase cars. He really just enjoyed the chase and had no intention of catching it; and if he ever did catch it, it would take him a while to figure out what to do with it.

Shortly after my father resigned as deacon and left the church, my mother asked to address the congregation one Sunday morning. Jennifer was witness to my mother's beautifully articulated and heartfelt apology for any part she had unwittingly played in the minor scandal that had shifted the church's focus away from its mission of worship and fellowship. She did not point fingers at anyone else, nor did she mention anyone else by name. She undoubtedly knew that some responsibility for her failed marriage lay at her own feet.

My parents' divorce was finalized in early 1983. As I had seen her do before, my mother faced the challenge head-on, knowing she must "get past this." She stayed busy, performing her various jobs in the church and leaning just the right amount on family, friends, and me. She firmly believed, and taught me as much, that the best way to weather a personal storm was to either involve oneself in a project or do something for other people. I remember coming home one weekend and finding that all of the kitchen cabinets had been taken down; within a few weeks they were stripped, repainted, and re-installed. I sensed she was methodically re-establishing her self-sufficiency. She obtained an old fifty-five-gallon drum and placed it in a dirt patch in the backyard to burn receipts and papers containing personal information. She bought a BB gun to keep pesky raccoons, opossums, and squirrels out of the yard. She wisely didn't try to do everything, however; if a chore that required climbing or heavy lifting was beckoning, she usually asked Jennifer's sweet husband, Thomas, for help or waited until I visited and allowed me to take care of it. During one of my visits, she asked if I would change out the broken flood lights on the back corner of her house. I told her I would be happy to, but out of curiosity asked what had happened to them. She grinned sheepishly and told me she had been shooting her BB gun "from the hip" at some varmint and accidentally took out the flood lights instead—we both got a good laugh out of that.

In the summer of 1983, she moved into Aunt Millie's apartment in Savannah, Georgia, and took a job in Housekeeping for a local Holiday Inn. Her leadership skills and strong work ethic were so obvious that after only a month she was asked to be the supervisor of Housekeeping. The other housekeepers were of various ethnicities, primarily from the lower economic strata, and had been working there much longer than my mother; yet they accepted her as their new supervisor with very little fuss. I believe that in the short time they had worked with her, they had observed her high standards and had deemed her fair and impartial. This didn't surprise me any because my mother had always been blind to ethnicity, socio-economic class, and appearance when taking stock of another human being. Dr. Martin Luther King, Jr., would have been proud of my mother because she truly did judge people on the "content of their character."

My mother actually gave thought to a permanent move to Savannah. She was fascinated with its rich history and, of course, her sister worked and lived there; but, toward the end of the summer in 1983, she became quite homesick. Since she had hitched a ride to Savannah with my aunt and didn't have her own car with her, she asked her dear friend Jennifer to come get her and take her back home. Being the wonderful friend that she was, Jennifer and one of her children went straight away to fetch my mother.

Over the Christmas holidays in 1983, my mother decided to join the family caravan to Winter Park, Colorado. Aunt Gail is a snow fanatic and had been the visionary behind the Adams family enjoying a white Christmas together. I thought that if anything could soothe my mother's broken heart it would be time with her beloved family in a magical place. My husband and I joined them later, flying out on Christmas Eve with plans to drive back to Alabama with my aunt and uncle after the holidays. The vast majority of my immediate Adams family—aunts, uncles, first cousins, and my grandmother were there; family friends Ms. Nita, her son Jay, and her niece were also included. There were three notable absences: my uncle Ralph, whom my aunt Millie had separated herself from two years earlier; cousin Steve, whom we had buried in April 1982, just twenty months before; and my father, who for all intents and purposes was now out of the family— the weight of sadness from those losses felt by each of us in different measure.

For the most part, however, we enjoyed our family time together that Christmas. We skied, rode snowmobiles, made snow angels, and drank hot chocolate while sitting by roaring fireplaces. We took a horse-drawn hayride, staying warm by snuggling close together under blankets and drifts of hay, to a prepared campsite a few miles away where we ate camp stew out of splatter-ware bowls inside a tent and roasted marshmallows on an open fire just outside. As for my mother, she was putting on a brave face and trying to live in the moment, but her heartbreak at times, at least to me, was palpable.

Following our vacation in Colorado during the 1983-84 Christmas and New Year's holiday season, we all returned to our respective homes, jobs, and lives—cousin Bebe back to New Orleans, Aunt Millie to Savannah, cousin Marygail back to Pensacola, and the rest of us back to various spots in Alabama.

Finally and mercifully, with the start of the 1984 school year in August, my mother obtained the bus aide position for which she had applied nearly five years earlier and officially began her second career. She discovered that a bus driver position had also come open for the 1984 school year, the job which she had been led to believe she was next in line for back in September 1983. Jennifer and I saw the infamous temper flare when my mother learned that the job had been given instead to a person whom my mother believed to have had a social relationship with a school system administrator. In accordance with her strong sense of right and wrong, she respectfully lodged her complaint with the very person whom she believed to have allowed a personal relationship to influence their professional decisions.

It seemed at first blush that the bus driver job in 1984 should have been awarded to my mother and served as a miscarriage of justice when it was given to someone else. But I have wondered over the years, as I am a direct product of her training, if a more divine force was in play during that sequence of events. Just maybe she wasn't yet healed enough at that time to focus her undivided attention on safely driving those precious children from point A to point B. So instead, she was awarded the aide job, the person who kept vigil over the frail children, riding in the back with them, close by, and able to render immediate assistance should it become necessary. Just maybe her needs at that time were more fully met by being so close to children who needed her and who would, in short order, grow to love her.

This example of divine timing reminds me of the Sunday School lesson I heard my mother teach years ago on Mary, Martha, and their brother Lazarus. The eleventh chapter of the Gospel of John records the story this way: Jesus was dear friends with Mary, her sister Martha, and their brother Lazarus. In verse five the Scripture specifically says that Jesus loved all three of them. As Lazarus lay ill in Bethany, his sisters sent word to Jesus saying, "Lord, the one you love is sick." When Jesus heard of Lazarus' illness, He waited two more days before He went to Bethany. Lazarus had been embalmed and entombed for four days. Both Mary and Martha said to Jesus, "Lord, if you had been here, my brother would not have died." Jesus asked to be taken to Lazarus's tomb. He was so moved by the sadness of Mary and Martha and others in the town that He himself wept. Jesus then proceeded to raise Lazarus from the dead. The divine truth illustrated by this great story and taught to me by my mother is that we humans want what we want, when we want it, and God sometimes appears to have missed His opportunity to help us attain it by arriving "four days late," when in fact his "arrival" is always right on time and we get what we need when we need it.

My mother found her aide job very satisfying, and I know she loved being in such close proximity to the children. I remember routinely seeing school pictures of the children on her bus and listening to her tell their stories. I told her many times that she was a better woman than I because I knew I didn't have the emotional strength to do what she was doing.

She worked as an aide for the next eight school years and in August 1992 was finally awarded a driver's job. Along with the driver's position, she inherited the bus aide, Ms. Phyllis. Phyllis was deeply southern and possessed a slight speech impediment that would cause her to pronounce a word such as "dollar" as "doll-ur-rin." She and my mother hit it off immediately as I am certain my mother made her feel loved and special. They made an excellent team, and my favorite Mom/Phyllis story is the one where they rose to the challenge of fashioning a back-up emergency escape plan for the children on the bus.

We are all familiar with the exits in the back of school buses that children can use in the event of an emergency. But Mom's bus was carrying children who were not always mobile and who would need assistance if evacuation became necessary concurrent with a loss of power to operate the lifts. One student was a teenaged boy, wheelchair-bound and quite heavy. Mom and Phyllis came up with the idea to use a heavy quilt to form a ramp out the back exit. Being the larger and stronger of the two women, my mom would maneuver the young man out of his wheelchair and onto about a third of the quilt. Then she would slide him to the exit and toss the remaining length of quilt out the back exit door to Phyllis. While Phyllis held the quilt firmly to the ground by standing on it, Mom would pull back on her third to keep the quilt taut, and the young man would slide safely to the ground via the quilt chute. Mom and Phyllis received high marks from their boss during their safety demonstration. When I heard the details, I couldn't help myself, I was so proud of her and congratulated her as if she had just kicked the winning field goal in an Alabama football game.

I was also extremely proud of her when during her tenure as bus driver the requirements for drivers were amped up by new state regulations and every driver had to obtain their CDL if they wished to keep their jobs. Mom passed the test with flying colors, only missing a couple of questions. I also remember her researching the missed questions to make sure she understood why she had missed them, and then re-learning the correct information.

With each passing year following the divorce my mother healed a little bit more—time, as only time can do, applying and reapplying the soothing balm. My husband and I visited her often, and she would sometimes drive down to Dothan to visit us. The three of us played golf together and occasionally vacationed together. Once we rented a two-bedroom condo at the beach in Florida and just spent easy quality time together. I remember us playing the game Trivial Pursuit and becoming highly suspicious when my mother answered the question, "What Latin phrase is attributed to Julius Caesar following his quick victory at the Battle of Zela around 47 b.c.?" My husband and I watched her appear to ponder the question and then heard her answer "Veni, vidi, vici." I narrowed my eyes, grinning, and looked at her sideways. That was, after all, the fourth straight answer she had gotten right. She could no longer keep a straight face and began giggling uncontrollably, which caused us to giggle also. She confessed that when my husband and I had taken a short bathroom break several minutes earlier, she had memorized every conceivable answer on the next five cards— mind you, not in an effort to win the game, but realizing she would eventually be called out for "knowing too much" and then we would all get a good laugh out of the prank.

I loved my mother's sense of humor. It was at times self-deprecating, like the time she asked to borrow my string bikini (I couldn't imagine why, but loaned it anyway). She took the thing to the Adult Sunday School Class swim party, and in front of several class members, clutching the tiny garments in one hand, asked where she could change. That brought uproarious laughter, except from my father, who didn't like being outdone in the humor department.

Mom dearly loved the comedy of Tim Conway, particularly his little old man routine, him taking dozens of tiny shuffling steps and mumbling something incoherent but obviously funny to Harvey Korman. She also enjoyed clumsy comedy such as the pratfalls of Laurel and Hardy. Sometimes she would find something hilariously entertaining that she would actually have to explain to me. A particular example was a small oil painting she once spotted at a gift shop of some birds sitting on a telephone wire looking down at people. The title was "Birdwatchers"—it cracked her up. She saw the play on words immediately, whereas it took me a while.

She had several expressions that were quite funny and she would use them often in her everyday speech. If as a passenger in a vehicle, she was providing an all clear signal for the driver, she would say, "Hit it, Otis" (I have no idea who Otis was). If she had a long list of things to do and needed to get on with it, she would excuse herself by saying, "I've got worms to scratch and eggs to lay." "You've got the cat's eye, kiddo," meant the light had turned green while I was daydreaming and it was safe to proceed. During a most satisfying yawn and stretch she would usually say, voice a little pinched from the motions, that she could stretch a mile if she didn't have to walk back.

She was also a very good sport and took my gentle teasing in stride. There were a few words that she pronounced oddly, and I couldn't resist poking a little fun at her. For example, gas for her car was pronounced "gyce." When I heard her use this word, I would say, giggling, "Mom, it's not 'gyce,' which rhymes with 'ice'; it's 'gas,' which rhymes with 'pass,' like 'pass gas.'" She would always respond good-naturedly, "Oh hush, girl, what do you know?" If she had done something two times, then she had done it "twiced," and "Walmart" was "Walmark's." In truth, I thought her mispronunciation of these words was adorable and I didn't really want her to change a thing.

Sometimes the tomboy in both of us would come out and we would wrestle, standing up, and see who could toss whom onto Mom's king-sized bed. The winner would always raise both arms in victory and pump the air a little, and both winner and loser would laugh heartily.

By far the most wonderful thing about my mother's sense of humor was the fact that she simply gave into it, allowing it to transform her face and body, which made her laughter nothing short of contagious. Her initial smile would grow into a broad and toothy grin; and what started out as audible and rhythmic ack-ack sounds from her core would soon turn inaudible and cause her to bend forward a little, visibly shaking, and most of the time crossing her legs to keep a little pee at bay.

My parents' brands of humor were very different. I never felt as if my mother desired to compete with my father for laughs, but rather was content to allow him the spotlight that he craved. My father was a masterful storyteller, replete with funny faces, voices, and gestures that only magnified the humor; with his well-honed sense of comedic timing, he could reduce any audience to a quivering mass of giggles. My mother, on the other hand, was not a showman and would have been uncomfortable in the center of all that attention. Whereas my mother would make light of herself for a laugh, my father would often make light of others, including my mom. My father would tell a risqué joke without consideration of his audience, whereas my mother's jokes, if they had a tinge of innuendo would be told only to a small gathering of friends or family. My father's humor could sometimes be cruel and sometimes was used as a veil for a personal jab. My mother was way too honest for such an indirect approach; and if she felt the need to give difficult or constructive feedback, she just gave it face to face.

On November 17, 1985, my grandmother Lucy turned eighty, and Aunt Gail threw her a huge surprise party. Mom was assigned the role of concocting a story to get my grandmother dressed up a bit and to the party spot without letting the cat out of the bag. The surprise was successful and my grandmother was inundated with attention and love from every living Adams relative I had ever heard of. It was also cathartic for my mom as she was able to see some aunts, uncles, and cousins for the first time since becoming single. As was only fitting, her extended family provided her with their love and support and understanding even though they loved my father.

The following year my grandmother Alta succumbed just a few short months after her eightieth birthday. She had suffered under the ravaging effects of Alzheimer's disease for approximately fifteen years; on August 9, 1986, pneumonia finally seized what was left of her life. The close-knit Collins family gathered in the hometown of Thorsby

to lay my grandmother to her well-deserved rest, and I saw my fath
again for the first time since I had sent him the awful letter. My moth
accompanied me to the funeral and, as she had done many times, set th
standard of behavior to which I aspire. My mother had taught me and
was exemplifying that there was never an excuse for being rude. She
grieved her ex-mother-in-law's passing and felt empathy for all of the
children, especially my father. She gave him her sincere condolences,
and we both embraced him, the weight of my father's loss and my
mother's exemplary behavior forming the foundation for the rebuilding
of my relationship with my dad.

Four months later on January 1, 1987, yet another member of the
Collins family, Aunt Helen, passed away. My mother, who had long
held a soft spot in her heart for the black sheep of the family, also
attended Aunt Helen's funeral. My father was barely consolable after the
death of his older sister, born number four of ten and chronologically
adjacent to him. My mother was completely empathetic. As she had
done at my grandmother's funeral, Mom once again expressed sadness
for my father's loss in a dignified and respectful manner.

My mother's classy behavior at the two public venues where she
and my father came face to face for the first time after their divorce had
done a great deal to help me realize that I had to take the first step to
repair the father-daughter relationship that I had foolishly risked in my
anger and immaturity. But nothing hits home like the realization that
you, yourself, are guilty of the very behavior for which you have self-
righteously judged someone else. Such was the case in late 1987, when
I met someone for whom I was most willing to sacrifice my marriage.
The judgment yardstick I had held up to measure my father's behavior
was now measuring me.

The only difference between his approach to divorce and mine, and
it provides me absolutely no solace, was that I told my husband why I
wished to end our marriage.

Upon hearing the news of my impending divorce, my precious
mother was at my side in no time offering her love and support. I
initially, and for many years thence, withheld the details behind my
decision to end my marriage from everyone except my mother. I told
her the unvarnished truth and then she and I held onto each other for

the longest time and cried together. That moment with my mother is the most authentic and most Christ-like expression of unconditional love in my entire life's experience. She did not condone, but neither did she condemn; she just loved.

I was single by early 1988 and coincidentally my job at the nuclear plant began to demand more and more of my time. I was actually supporting the control room, which involved rotating shifts, and often I was scheduled to work on various holidays. At least once per year and sometimes twice, each unit would be shut down for a refueling outage. Outages were scheduled for between thirty and forty days and required twelve-hour rotating shift work. During the years 1988 to 1992 I wasn't able to spend as much time with my family as I would have liked; even on off days I was too worn out to make the drive home. My mother was so faithful to visit me at my home in Dothan. Just spotting her car coming up my driveway never failed to provide me with a rush of sweet emotion.

In keeping with her car-loving nature, she had purchased a nice used third-generation Mustang convertible and drove with the top down as often as possible. I love the story of her first (and only) speeding ticket while driving the Mustang. After being stopped, she flirtatiously told the officer, a handsome young man, that she was guilty as charged, to which he responded, "Well, you almost look too good in that car for me to give you a ticket, but I have to do my job."

My mom didn't always roll over that easily when given a traffic citation, however, so I chalked it up to the officer's good looks. Once while living in Titusville she was issued a ticket for speeding in a school zone. That the ticket was issued for that reason just added insult to injury because my mother loved children and would have never been reckless with their safety. She honestly believed that the signage had not been displayed properly and therefore she was unaware that she had entered a school zone. She decided to fight it. With her characteristic thoroughness, she prepared her defense. She scripted and practiced what she would say to the judge and even sketched out a small diagram of the school, the road, and the signage. When the moment of truth arrived, my well-prepared mother went mute under the glare of the robed judge, elevated above everyone on his bench. He looked down at her and asked her what she had to say for herself, and all she could muster was "Nothing, Your Honor." She recounted that the whack of the gavel and the booming voice of the judge declaring the case dismissed brought her out of her stupor, but by then it was too late. When telling this story, Mom would always end it with another of her favorite little ditties, "He who hesitates is lost."

In addition to her visits to my home in Dothan, she also routinely mailed funny and encouraging cards to me. The minute I had the envelope in my hand, I would tear into it, pleasantly anxious to see it and read it. Even if she hadn't put her return address on the envelope, I would have recognized the large looping script as coming from her hand. There would always be a short note written inside the card. Sometimes her cursive capital "S" would be turned into a little duck, a beak and an eye looking right added to the top loop and web feet added to the bottom loop. The note usually contained a brief sentence about what she was up to and would always end with "I Love You, Darling, Mom."

My mother absolutely loved standing in the card aisle reading the cards. She could stand there, for what seemed like an hour or more, taking her time to choose just the right one, be it for me or someone else. She especially delighted in reading the funny cards, sometimes exploding into laughter at the punchline. She usually sent occasion cards, but she also sent cards for no reason other than to tell me she loved me. My refrigerator would usually have a card from her magnetically affixed to the door, where it would stay as a comforting memento until I received the next one.

In 1992 I was given a much welcomed opportunity to work as a loaned employee to the Institute of Nuclear Power Operations in Atlanta, Georgia. Loanee assignments to this organization are typically between fifteen and twenty-four months long and require a relocation to the Atlanta area. So I sold my Dothan home and set up housekeeping, albeit temporarily, in a two-bedroom apartment about seven miles from INPO headquarters. (Author's note: INPO is an organization established in 1979 by the U. S. nuclear power industry in response to recommendations by the Kemeny Commission Report following the investigation of the Three Mile Island accident. The organization sets industry-wide performance objectives, criteria, and guidelines for nuclear power plant operations that are intended to promote operational excellence and improve the sharing of operational experience between nuclear power plants. INPO is funded entirely by the U. S. nuclear industry.)

Although my new assignment required significant travel, my mom and I saw each other regularly, fitting visits in between my travel weeks. Sometimes she would drive to Atlanta and sometimes I would travel to her. During my fifteen months in Atlanta, Mom began to experience a very irritating malady, which we learned later to be trigeminal neuralgia, more commonly referred to as Tic Douloureux. Her main symptom was a sudden, severe, electric-shock-like pain on one side of her face. Her pain would come in unannounced, intermittent episodes that lasted only a few seconds and could be brought on by eating or brushing her teeth or even just allowing cold air to hit her face. I remember her telling me that if it lasted any longer than a few seconds it would literally be unbearable. True to character, Mom did her homework, researching her symptoms in a medical encyclopedia and, finding a match, wondered if it might be trigeminal neuralgia. The encyclopedia explained that even though the cause was unknown, there were several theories as to how the trigeminal nerve becomes affected. One theory involved historical facial trauma. My mom recollected two such events. The first caused a deep cut to one corner of her mouth when as a child she was struck by a jagged-topped tin can my grandmother had innocently tossed over her shoulder to get it out of their yard. In the second event she had been inadvertently struck on the mouth by a softball over four decades earlier. When the professional diagnosis matched my mom's layman diagnosis, she was placed on a drug called carbamazepine. The drug did its job as far as relieving the symptoms, but soon it became evident to both of us that a side effect was a change in my mother's behavior, causing her to be anxious about situations she had previously handled with ease. When we found ourselves in a significant traffic jam after attending the Laser Show at Stone Mountain, Georgia, my intrepid mother (whose only fear that I was ever aware of was water and that was due to an insensitive uncle who foolishly held her under when she was a child) displayed uncharacteristic angst about our ability to navigate through the traffic to my apartment. This episode convinced us that some other form of treatment was necessary.

After consultation with a neurosurgeon at the University of Alabama Medical Center in Birmingham, she decided to take the surgical route to permanently relieve her pain and allow her to stop taking the carbamazepine. During the neurosurgeon's explanation of the procedure, we both cringed at the details. Basically, he would bore a quarter-sized hole at the base of her skull on the side where her pain was being experienced, then lift her brain a little—at this point, Mom quipped, "If you find one"—and then trace the trigeminal nerve to determine exactly what was interfering with it. He went on to explain the surgery had a very good success rate and further predicted that the worse thing she would have to deal with following surgery would be a king-sized headache. He did not exaggerate.

Following surgery, he came to me in the waiting room and told me that all had gone according to plan and that he had found the trigeminal nerve butted up against a blood vessel. He explained that he simply wrapped the nerve in surgical "felt" and put everything back in place—oh, the wonders of modern medicine. She did have the king-sized headache he had predicted, but once she weathered that, this particular challenge was behind her.

The year 1993 was a difficult one for my mother, as that twelve-month span bracketed her first bout with breast cancer, my cousin Gary's suicide, and the passing of her mother in October, rounding out the one-two-three punch. I was actually in San Luis Obispo, California, on a business trip when I received news of my grandmother's passing and flew home immediately to be with my family.

My grandmother had been loved by many, many people, including family, in-laws, and a wide variety of friends ranged in age from her peers to people generations younger. Her health, which to my recollection had always been quite good, had begun to deteriorate several months earlier when she developed COPD-style symptoms that had us all quite worried. My cousin Marygail was actually able to be nursemaid for our grandmother, which allowed her to stay out of the hospital for the most part and be cared for in her home, the one she had shared with Aunt Gail and Uncle Gary for the last thirty-five years. My grandmother passed on October 10, 1993, just thirty-eight days shy of her eighty-eighth birthday.

I was deeply saddened by her death, as were all of her grandchildren. She had been uniquely able to love all of us as we were, so to speak. She was able to home in on what each of us was good at and praise us for it. I never heard her make comparisons between us, comparisons which inevitably would leave someone holding the short straw. I imagined that she was now in heaven and again seeing my grandfather, the love of her life. I had always pictured theirs to have been a uniquely good marriage, measuring it by certain descriptions I had heard over the years—for example, my mother recounting that she never saw them argue; she knew they did, from time to time, but they always took the discussion behind closed doors, out of eye- and earshot of their children. I heard my grandmother tell many times, with a look of joy on her face, of the sweet description my grandfather would give of her during their courtship—"hair black as jet, and eyes as blue as the sky." Although my grandmother's death left a non-fillable hole in our family, I was happy for my grandparents' long-awaited reunion.

The news that my mother at age sixty-six had been diagnosed with breast cancer came as a shock to me. Even though efforts to raise awareness had been going strong for several years, I ignorantly thought of breast cancer as a "younger woman's disease," when in fact it is no respecter of persons and the risk of developing it actually increases with age. In my mother's case, there was good news, however. The tumor, as the doctor put it, was "atypical." It was just the opposite of the aggressive, fast-growing tumors that defined breast cancer in those days, but was instead a lethargic, slow-growing mass. I remain convinced that somehow the propensity had lain dormant in my mother's system until it was awakened and nourished by the regimen of post-menopausal hormones the medical profession had advised to counter the natural loss of estrogen. Be that as it may, it was a new challenge, and she faced it with characteristic resolve.

The oncologist gave Mom two options for treatment. The first, a lumpectomy, would be far less invasive, would require some radiation but no chemotherapy, and would render her a 95 percent chance of never having to deal with it again. The second option was the mastectomy. This route would require no radiation nor chemotherapy and would give her a 99 percent chance of no further cancer. Mom and I basically disagreed on the two options, But, as it was neither my body nor my decision to make, I acquiesced to my mother's choice for mastectomy.

Following the successful surgery, I took some time off from work and cared for my mother at her home. I performed post-operative tasks that I never thought I would have the strength to do, including routinely emptying her drainage pump. It seemed only fitting that I be there and care for her because she had done it for me countless times before. As exemplified by my mother over my entire life, when you love somebody you bring up the strength from somewhere to do what must be done.

The breast cancer took a little wind out of my mom's sails; but in due time, she righted. She purchased a prosthetic breast and began the process of getting used to the heavy mound, strapped tightly against the scar tissue on her chest. The first time I saw it we were in her bedroom; she was changing out of church clothes and into comfy house clothes when she removed it from her bra and tossed it to me, giggling. "Oh dear!" I exclaimed as I caught the thing in mid-air, judging its heft to be akin to that of a small medicine ball. One thing was for sure, my mother had not let breast cancer take away her wonderful sense of humor.

In the mid-1990s she decided to start dating again, and I did not like it one iota. My friends criticized me for not being more supportive, reminding me that my mother was a big girl, could take care of herself, and still had a lot to offer someone in a relationship, all of which was indeed true. But no matter how hard they teased me, I could not reconcile myself to support the idea. As for my mother, she was interested in companionship, someone to have dinner with, converse with, and play golf with. But all I could envision was some old man trying to take advantage of her—probably akin to the way she felt when I first started dating.

In 1994, after my INPO assignment in Atlanta had ended, I moved to a small farm in south Georgia, an hour's driving distance from the nuclear plant. For the next two years I once again was working rotating shifts, this time as a Shift Supervisor for Unit 1. In our six-week shift rotation there was always a four-day break Thursday through Sunday;

those four-day weekends were the only reasonable time for Mom and me to visit each other in person. My south Georgia farm home was two hundred miles from mom's residence, and most of that route was two-lane highway. It was a tough drive and certainly untenable for a short weekend visit. Even though we didn't see each other as much as we would have liked, we telephoned each other routinely during those two years, sharing the events of our lives in vivid detail. My typical pose for a phone call with my mom was sprawled across my bed, up on elbows, holding the phone to my ear. After just a few minutes of listening I would be swept up into the easy, back-and-forth flow of words and details that had virtually always been the hallmark of our personal communications.

During one such phone call, Mom shared the details of a date she had recently been on. I squeezed my eyes shut against the image but was determined to be a good listener. My mother believed that being a good listener did not come naturally to very many people and was a skill that had to be developed. As a child, she taught me this little poem:

> The wise old owl lived in an oak.
> The more he heard, the less he spoke.
> The less he spoke, the more he heard.
> Why can't we all be like that wise old bird?

She believed that good listeners were rare, and that really listening to someone tell their story was like giving them a gift—a gift, she would say, "more precious than gold."

So, with eyes shut and ears open, I gave my undivided attention as she walked me through the details of her night out with this fellow, whom, I might add, I did not know. Apparently and probably wisely, she had told him that she would drive and pick him up for their evening out. Sometime during the date, he brazenly scooted closer to her in the car and put his arm on her shoulder, allowing his wrist and hand to dangle, hovering just above her breast. As he allowed his fingers to gently rest there, he asked her if that felt good. My magnificent mother responded, "It probably would, if that one was real." My laughter exploded into the receiver, causing me to roll over off of my elbows and onto my back. I remember thinking to myself, "I love this woman!" My friends had been right—my mother could definitely take care of herself. And as for her foray back into the dating world—well, let's just say, that was that.

The dating incident was not the first time my mother had used her sense of humor to put someone back in place. I love the story of the playful Dr. S., Ms. Nita's gentleman friend in the late 1990s, jumping into the pool at Ms. Nita's house, then taking his swim trunks off underwater, and tossing them onto the pool deck. My mom was lounging in the pool at the time; when she heard Jay, sitting in a nearby lounge chair, exclaim, "Oh, my Lord!" she opened her eyes in time to see the trunks flying through the air and hitting the concrete with a wet splat. She immediately got out of the pool and headed into the house. Dr. S. pleaded, "Don't go, Kathryn," to which my mother replied, "I don't want to be in a pool with that dead thing floating around in it."

In 1994 John Berendt's first book, *Midnight in the Garden of Good and Evil,* was published and became a *New York Times* Best-Seller for 216 weeks. I knew very little about its content, only that it was reportedly a very entertaining historical account of Savannah, Georgia. Based on my mother's interest in the eccentric southern town, I recommended the book to her—lesson learned, never recommend a book to your mother that you haven't already read.

The telephone call I received from Mom following her initial encounter with this highly recommended work of non-fiction began curtly, to say the least. I answered the phone and immediately heard my name, no "Hello," no "Hi, honey," just my name. It was spoken in that way all children, no matter their age, recognize from their parent's mouth as the beginning of a rebuke. I couldn't imagine why my mother would be upset with me. I tuned in even closer to ensure I caught every detail of her diatribe. It began with a question, "Have you read this book?" "No, ma'am, not yet," I answered softly. Those were my last sounds for several minutes as she proceeded to talk non-stop. I'm not even certain she took a breath. She continued, in staccato, "Well— it— is— awful! These characters are saying things that I cannot believe anyone would even say, much less do." And then, to my horror, she read me the offending sentences. Just hearing such carnal, street language emanate from my precious mother's mouth was a total affront to my image of her. Mentally, I was once again a child, holding my flattened palms over each ear and saying rapidly, out loud to myself, "Lalalalalalalala," drowning out the offensive sounds. Finally, she took a breath. In that conversational pause, I began a litany of apologies, explaining that I should never have recommended it without knowing more about it and how sorry I was that it had offended her. I said, "Mom, just throw that darn book away and don't read another page." Then, silence. The ensuing dead air made me wonder if I had lost the connection. Finally, my mother said softly, "I don't think I can." At this, peals of laughter burst onto the line simultaneously from both directions. What had started out as the most unpleasant conversation I had ever had with her soon righted itself and put us back on familiar ground—laughing together—all thanks to her ability to allow humor to sometimes trump decorum.

As my reader knows from past chapters, my mother may have been a bit Victorian when it came to the subject of sex, but was far from being a full-blown prude. She simply viewed sexual relations as a rite of passage for married people and saw it as an important part of a sacred Biblical union; therefore, the vulgar verbs and nouns used to describe the equipment and the mechanics of sex were never a part of her lexicon. She viewed casual, reckless, or uncommitted sexual relations as almost always a losing proposition for the female involved.

When it came to foul language, my mother's vocabulary was limited but effective enough. Her curse words of choice were those of the southern gentry, defined by the fact that they could be found in the Bible. *Damnation, hell,* and *jackass* (her name for poor drivers) were her go-to words when no other word would do. The only other foul language my mother ever used was the *sh* word, but that was extremely rare. Most of the time when tempted to use that word, she would pause for what seemed like an eternity on the *sh* sound, stretching it to the breaking point, trying to calm herself down in the interim, and finally culminating with *sssssshhhhhhhhhhhh-asta!*

In 1996, Mom's sister Millie retired from her long-time job in Savannah with a biomedical company and moved into my mother's house. Their co-habitation was a decent arrangement and would have been an excellent arrangement had it not been for my aunt's propensity to collect things. She paid a small rent, took care of her part of the phone bill, and had her own bedroom and bathroom—not to mention her own elbow room, which she systematically filled with stuff. The most obvious example of her tendency to collect was the multiple clear storage bins stacked in her bedroom from floor to ceiling and spilling over into the living room, crammed full of every species of Beanie-Baby known to mankind. It was just shy of creepy because there were very few spots in the house where one could get away from the little backsides, legs, eyes, and smiling mouths that pressed against every square inch of the bins. To accommodate my aunt's growing collections, my mother asked Jennifer's husband, Thomas, to enclose the small patio at the back of Mom's house. She decided she would move her treasured desk to the new space, which was not air-conditioned nor heated, and allow my aunt to have more room for storage inside. It worked for a while, but soon my aunt's boxes and wrapping paper and paraphernalia took over half of the newly enclosed patio. In truth, the resulting cramped quarters probably bothered me more than my mother because I never once heard my mother complain about her younger sister's idiosyncrasies.

Going places and having fun with dear friends and family had always been a feature of my mother's life, those fun times evident in scores of photographs she had kept through the years. My mother's family was chiefly a matriarchal clan, consisting primarily of steel magnolias and modern day Amazons more than willing to share their life with a good man but determined to never be totally dependent nor subservient to him. This core of strong-willed Adams women attracted other strong females over the years and slowly grew into a large circle of friends who were linked by their shared histories, their character, and their genuine love for each other. This group included my mom, my aunts, their dear friends, friends of those dear friends, former workmates, my cousins, Ms. Nita, and her sister Nelda. They would gather multiple times a year in various places to attend events, play cards and board games, eat together, and laugh, mostly laugh. Each member of this "group of girls" was the face of a much larger family that, like all families over time, experienced both highs and lows. When a new baby was born into one of the families, or a graduate was accepted to the college of his choice, or someone got a new job, the entire group would celebrate. By the same token, when an illness was diagnosed or a loved one lost, the entire group would pray and mourn. Theirs was a collective of relationships where each member could multiply their personal joys and divide their deepest sorrows simply by sharing. Occasionally I was in their midst and marveled at the sheer joy that filled the air surrounding them, everyone talking at the same time, the non-stop conversations punctuated by periodic explosions of laughter. In August 2003 I invited the group to my lake home in Eufaula, Alabama, for a long weekend. The weekend coincided with my cousin Bebe's forty-eighth birthday and we had a grand time eating, playing games, and celebrating. Bebe had bought Rosie the Riveter tee-shirts for everyone, and we took a number of photographs to mark the occasion. Bebe thought Rosie the perfect mascot for this strong group of women.

Over the next few years, while I was engaged in a demanding career and lived over two hundred miles away, I gave thanks more than once for this special group and also for Ms. Ellen and Jennifer. I believed that between me and them, my mother couldn't help but know how much she was loved and treasured, and I knew without question they would look out for her.

In 1998 Mom retired from her bus driver's job after fourteen years of service. The job had been a life-saver for her, not so much for the small additional income, but for the fact she was giving of herself to young people who needed her. She left a legacy of dedication and caring, and I was so very proud of her for that.

In 1999, along about the time Mom's precious friend Ellen passed away, I sold my farm home in Georgia and moved back to Alabama. In 2000 I bought a lake lot on Lake Eufaula, a 45,000-acre man-made lake named after the town it bordered, and began construction on a home there in mid-2001. For several months while the home was being built, I lived in a one-bedroom duplex located between the construction site and the nuclear plant. It was in this duplex that I had my private time of grieving following the tragedy known as "9-11." Such an event causes one to want to hear the voices of the people they love. My mother was my first phone call.

Later, in 2001 Mom was once again diagnosed with breast cancer—the 99 percent chance had been a miscalculation. It was the same brand of cancerous tumor, slow growing and lethargic in nature, but cancer all the same. This time the treatment decision was a simple one; the mastectomy on the other breast actually aided her balance as she had long before then stopped wearing the prosthesis unless she absolutely had to.

Around that time Mom was also dealing with a few other conditions. She had high blood pressure and elevated cholesterol and took a daily regimen of pills for each condition. The disease that I worried about the most, however, was the type 2 diabetes. She was about thirty pounds heavier than she needed to be, and her old friend sugar had become enemy number one. I can recall only one instance in our shared history when I became extremely frustrated with her.

My frustration centered on her lackadaisical approach to eating right and exercising once she was diagnosed with type 2 diabetes. My fussing was certainly not doing the trick; so I soon stopped all that and began focusing solely on encouraging her to eat right and exercise, to somewhat better results.

With 20/20 hindsight I can see that the series of physical challenges my mother faced in the last nine years of her life were piling up, and in the aggregate these challenges were telling me as early as 2002 that the time she spent alone should probably be minimized. But it was events between 2002 and 2005 that finally got my attention and moved me to action.

5

By early 2002 I had moved into the new lake house and almost concurrently received a promotion to Plant Assistant General Manager. My new job brought with it increased responsibility but a small reduction in the day-to-day type stress that had been a feature of my previous assignment. My new job also called for more face-to-face interaction with people from our other plants in Georgia and with various corporate departments in Birmingham. The resulting work travel between my home in Eufaula and our headquarters in Birmingham always took me directly by my mother's house, and I took those opportunities to look in on my mom.

I clearly remember my first peek inside my mother's slowly altering mind. After attending a work meeting in Birmingham in mid-2002, I decided to stop by my mother's house and pay her a surprise visit. As I made the turn onto the dirt road, I could already see that my mother's green Ford Explorer was not in the driveway. But my aunt Millie's car was there; so I decided to stop and see if perhaps Mom was running an errand and was expected to return soon. My aunt said Mom had gone to the drugstore to have some prescriptions refilled and added that she had been gone for quite a while. I decided to wait for her, but as five minutes turned into ten and ten into fifteen, I became anxious and decided to drive into town to make sure she was okay. My aunt confirmed the pharmacy for me; so off I went. About ten minutes later I pulled into the parking lot and seeing Mom's SUV there, breathed a small sigh of relief. I pulled into the empty space adjacent to her car and parked. As soon as I was inside the store, I began scanning right and left looking for my mother's pretty head of gray-white hair over the tops of the aisles. Seeing no sign of her, I walked toward the pharmacy section and saw her sitting alone in one of the waiting chairs. I said excitedly, "Hey, Mom!" She answered just as excitedly, "Hey, baby!" I continued, "What are you waiting for, sweetie?" "You," she replied. I giggled. I knew that couldn't be right because my visit was a surprise, but I dismissed it, chalking the answer up to her quick wit. I looked toward the pharmacist and raised my eyebrows as a way of asking if Mom was waiting on her prescription. The kind lady pharmacist shook her head and said she thought Mom was waiting for someone. She likely had a keener sense of what was going on than I did at that point.

During a drive-by visit in 2003, I found my mother at home, sitting in her favorite chair, watching television, and, as always, very happy to see me. As we chatted about this and that, she suddenly interjected, "The nicest man bought my breakfast at the Cracker Barrel." My ears perked up like a Doberman's and I asked quizzically, "Well, that was nice; did you not have enough money to pay, Momma?" "No," she said. I checked her wallet and indeed it was empty of cash. I reasoned that perhaps she had spent it all on groceries or gas and had just forgotten to replenish before venturing out. So my short-term fix was to remind her that she had a VISA card, and I coaxed her to keep it in her wallet at all times because in almost every case it was just as good as cash. I also made sure she had several bills in her wallet before I left that day and told her to let me know if she was ever short on cash. She promised me she would.

I was mildly concerned that she had obviously ventured out without money, but I was more concerned about how far she had ventured without money. The nearest Cracker Barrel was at least thirty miles away; so I came up with what I believed to be a good long-term solution. I knew Mom's favorite meal of the day was breakfast, and I also knew she loved to eat at the small, locally-owned diner near her house that actually served good food at all three meals of the day; so I coaxed her to have breakfast there when she had the urge to eat out. I further promised her that she wouldn't have to worry about paying for it because I would set up an account for her with the restaurant's management. I spoke with the ladies at the restaurant and asked if they minded simply debiting her account, including a tip for her waitress, each time she came in; and in turn I would check on her balance regularly and keep them whole. They were extremely kind, many of them knowing my mother by name and readily agreed to my proposal.

The only down side to this plan that I could imagine was that occasionally my father ate at the same restaurant. But I didn't see any reason that my mother's classy behavior toward him should change, and in fact it never did. However, during one of my visits with him, he reported on her and described in detail her behavior as he had obviously watched her eat breakfast at a distant table. He said she had taken several of the little tubs of half-and-half used for coffee, peeled back the little foil covers, and drank them. He also reported that she did pretty much the same thing with the small rectangular containers of various flavored jellies in a little stack on the table. I listened for an ounce of sympathy in his story and, finding none, allowed a little swoosh of anger to flow past the pilot light that always burned protectively in my heart for my beloved mother. Understanding full well that I had almost destroyed my relationship with my father in the past, however, and trying to be true to my mother's example, I swallowed back the disappointment, thanked him for the information, and politely found a reason to immediately leave his company.

On my drive home from my father's house that day, I thought more about her drinking the half-and-half and eating the jellies; and even though I didn't appreciate his insensitive delivery of the information, it was valuable nonetheless. A quick internet search told me that her behavior was symptomatic of the type 2 diabetes she was dealing with and that it could be an indicator that either her medicines were no longer strong enough or that she was not taking the medicines as prescribed. Since she regularly saw her doctors regarding all of her health challenges, I assumed that she was not taking her medicines on time or perhaps—what I feared most—she was absent-mindedly skipping them altogether.

Again I called on the power of the internet and searched for a possible solution. I soon found a nifty device that would allow me to preload several days' worth of meds and would give Mom physical access to only the pills she was to take, either morning, noon, or evening for a specific day. It had a simple battery driven timer that caused the circular storage tray to rotate one space at a predesignated time. When the tray rotated, a small cutout in the lid settled precisely over a single little bin that I had earlier filled with the appropriate pills. It even had an alarm to alert Mom that it had in fact rotated and that it was time to take some meds. As soon as she tipped the device and emptied the pills into her palm, the alarm would silence. I placed the little device squarely in the middle of her kitchen on a butcher block she had to walk past several times a day to and from the bathroom. When I visited, I would always unlock the lid and ensure the previous weeks' pills had been taken and then reload the device for the upcoming week. Sometimes while I was visiting her, I would observe her habitually check the little bin by placing a finger in it to ensure it was empty. I gave myself a mental high-five and crossed my fingers, hoping this would continue to be a viable long-term solution.

In early January 2004 I received an offer to take a different position within my company. This time the new job was actually located at corporate headquarters in Birmingham. Although I was honored to be asked, I did not relish leaving my new home. But, as the old saying goes, it was an offer I couldn't refuse. The up-side was certainly the closer proximity to my mother. With help from the company's relocation policy, I was also able to purchase a moderate brick home in the suburbs of Birmingham, while still holding on to my lake house in Eufaula. My mother had always taught me that everything happened for a reason, and as if to lay testament to her teaching, the reason behind my unexpected move to Birmingham became crystal clear in the ensuing months.

The first of two clarifying events that helped me finally grasp the extent of my mother's diminishing capacity occurred on Memorial Day 2004. It was a long holiday weekend, and I had planned to spend part of it with my mother. In fact, I had planned to take her to eat barbeque, one her all-time favorites. I stopped by her house to pick her up. While we were visiting and chatting about life, she once again came out of nowhere with a statement similar to the one she had produced months earlier about the Cracker Barrel breakfast some "nice man" had paid for. She said, "I wish I could find that lady and give her back that twenty dollars that she gave me." I dropped my head in minor exasperation and then turned to look at her. "What's that, Mom?" I asked. I continued, "Sweetie, are you not keeping money in your wallet? Don't you still have your VISA card?" "No, and my VISA did not work," she answered. I checked her wallet and again found no cash, but I did find the VISA card. I was confused as to why it had not worked. So I began going through the storage compartment between the front seats of her Explorer looking for receipts and found amongst the scraps of paper and bits of detritus that tend to eventually fill a glove compartment an old expired VISA card. I reasoned that she had attempted to pay for gas with the expired card and had not thought to look in her wallet for a different one. I went back into the house and, thinking it would be a simple task, told my mother that we would find this lady and pay her back. My mom was very pleased. So I asked the obvious next question, "Where can we find her, Mom?" "At the Chevron station," she replied.

Over the next few hours, details of this woman and her likely whereabouts came out of my mother's mind in small bits, as if the facts were riding in separate chairs on a ferris wheel and were only intermittently accessible to her. I learned the woman's first name was Cathy (I think my mother eventually remembered this because her own name was Kathryn) and that she worked at a Chevron with "stalls." As my mother offered this particular detail, she would hold her beautiful hands about two feet apart and in karate-chop fashion bring them down, simultaneously stating the word "stalls." I eventually realized she was creating the car lanes adjacent to the gas pumps with her hands. I did not immediately pick up on the significance of this clue, reasoning that all gas stations were constructed that way, but over the next three hours it became apparent.

My early assumption was that she meant the closest Chevron, located about five miles from her house; so I asked her if it was the Chevron just south of town. She told me yes it was; so we headed off in that direction. As I pulled into the station a few minutes later, she offered, "This isn't it, honey." "Oh, okay," I said and then countered, "Is it the one in town?" "Yes," she said. Then we followed the road into the heart of town, where I knew there was another Chevron station. As we approached that station, she began to shake her little head side to side; and I realized without her having to say it that this was not the one. "Mom, is it the Chevron further south, down the four-lane?" "Yes," she answered. So off we went. The next closest Chevron was about twenty miles south and located on the northbound side of the four-lane, visible to us well before we exited. I pointed to the left, "Is that it, Mom?" "Yes," she replied. It was at that moment that she produced the lady's name. Mom said, "Her name is Cathy." "Great, Mom, that's good," I said. I pulled up to the station, parked the car, and told my mother I would be right back. I told her that if Cathy wasn't working I would try to find out what her schedule was so that we could ensure she got her money back. Mom said, "Well, you can go in there, but this isn't the one." I laughed out loud and honestly began to wonder if we would ever find this mysterious, generous Cathy. I decided, that since I was already stopped, I could at least go in and ask the person working if they knew a "Cathy" who also worked there. The gentleman attending the station was most kind and very understanding when I briefly explained the details of our mission. He told me that no one named Cathy worked at his station, but that he would be happy to check the schedule because the Chevrons in the vicinity were owned by the same people and the schedule was a common tool used by all of them. I told him that would be wonderful and simultaneously crossed my fingers. To my delight, there was one lady named Cathy who worked at another Chevron, nine miles further south and just off the four-lane. I thanked him effusively, returned to the car, and told Mom that I might have a lead on Cathy's whereabouts.

The moment I spotted the Chevron, the "stalls" clue was self-evident. It was a very modern station with a huge plaza of concrete in front of the Food Mart and chock-full of orderly and symmetrically arranged "stalls." I winked at Mom, told her to wish me luck, got out of the car, and went inside. I asked the lady attendant, whose name tag promised she was not our Cathy, if someone by that name worked there and told her why I wished to know. She said yes and, in fact, Cathy was due to report to work at 2 p.m. I glanced at my watch and saw that it was ten minutes before 2 p.m. I thanked her and returned to the car and told Mom the good news.

Eight minutes later, a car, once maroon in color but now blotchy and faded with age, came coughing and rattling into the plaza. It slowly made its way to the side of the station where I supposed employees would park, and something just told me it was she. Moments later, a diminutive middle-aged woman exited the car and with a noticeable limp slowly made her way to the front door. She was wearing the uniform of an attendant. With a lump the size of a golf ball in my throat, I called out to her, "Cathy, are you Cathy?" "I am," she answered, looking over at me. I said, "Cathy, do you remember this woman?" stepping aside to allow her to look into the passenger seat and see my mother. "Yes, I do," she said happily. I said, "Cathy, I am so grateful for your kindness, and we have come to repay you." She and my mother touched hands and smiled at each other, and I felt that lump in my throat again. As my eyes moistened, I thought to myself, "If there was anyone who could least afford to give up a twenty-dollar bill to a complete stranger it was this woman; yet she did it anyway." When she and my mother finished exchanging thank-yous and you're-welcomes, I followed Cathy to the door of the Food Mart to open it for her, gave her the money, and offered my own final thanks. She looked up at me and said, "I was very worried about your mother that day." "Yes, ma'am, I understand," I said self-consciously. This total stranger had flipped a switch for me, and I knew then and there that I had to take quick action to keep my mother off the road.

After that Memorial Day event, it became quite easy to imagine disturbing scenarios featuring my mother coming to harm because of her propensity to drive for miles without money or without gas in her car. I had been resistant to the signals for the last several months and despised the thought of singularly judging her capacity. I realized the most substantial part of my resistance to taking action had been my own denial that my heroine was in decline. I had always admired my mother's abilities behind the wheel and furthermore saw her car as a symbol of her independence and self-sufficiency, a hallmark of her very being. It was extremely difficult to imagine myself in the role of denying her anything, especially access to her car keys.

Although I cannot recall the source from which I learned of the professional assistance available from the Driving section of the Occupational Therapy Clinic at the UAB Medical Center, I can easily recall the compassion and professionalism of the staff there. I explained to Mom on our drive to Birmingham that we were going to a place equipped to help us understand if it was still safe for her to drive. She made no protestations. Our therapist looked to be about 8.99 months pregnant, and I said a silent prayer of thanks for my mother's training in obstetrics, albeit over fifty years ago. I figured, if push came to shove, some of that training would surely come back to her, giving me time to fetch "hot water and towels."

The young therapist explained that the examination would consist of a series of tests; if Mom did well on the first two, then the third would be an actual driving test in downtown Birmingham. I was allowed to observe the process from a few feet away and silently cheered her on. The first test Mom tackled was a static test requiring the use of a pencil to draw an unbroken line connecting numbered dots scattered willy-nilly on a piece of white paper. It appeared to me that she had done okay on that test. Next came the dynamic test. It was a computer-driven exercise designed to test Mom's ability to react to newly introduced stimuli in a timely manner. For this test, she was instructed to look straight at the middle of the screen, which was representative of her driving a vehicle. Next, small car and truck symbols would intermittently appear on the edge of the screen and "drive" toward her. Her job was to tell the therapist immediately upon sighting whether it was a car or a truck and from which direction it was coming. The two tests took no more than thirty minutes, and at the conclusion of the testing, our therapist stepped into another room to compile her findings. Mom and I waited for her return in relative silence.

A few moments later she re-entered the room, and although unable to sit comfortably because of her condition, she managed to find a non-judgmental posture and began talking to my mother. It went something like this: "Ms. Collins, in the short time you have been here with me, I have made the judgment that you are a very kind person and would never intentionally harm anyone or anything. But, Ms. Collins, you did not do well on our tests, and it tells me that if you continue to drive you could accidentally harm someone. If a small child or even a dog were to dart out in front of you, my tests tell me that you would likely not react quickly enough to avoid hitting them. Ms. Collins, I believe that would sadden you, no end." "Brilliant," I thought. This young lady had read my mother perfectly. I watched from the corner of my eye as she spoke and saw that my mother never broke eye contact with the young therapist and soon began gently nodding her head in acquiescence. It was a bittersweet moment for Mom and me, and I suspect for the young professional as well.

At the conclusion of her report, we thanked our young friend, gathered our purses, and headed for the parking deck. Once outside, I tucked my arm into the crook of my mother's and leaned a little bit toward her as we walked. I said, "Mom, I am so sorry that you cannot drive anymore." She responded, "Oh, honey, all good things come to an end." I felt the tightness in the roof of my mouth and blinked back the little pools that threatened to form in my eyes. Determined to not make this day any sadder than it already was, I asked her what she would like to do for the rest of the day and promised we would do anything she wished. She pondered the question for a few seconds and then announced, "Well, I would like some little Krystals and a cold beer." I burst into laughter and squeezed her even closer as we continued the walk to my car.

My assignment to the corporate office in January 2004 had definitely turned out to be a blessing in disguise as it kept me within an hour of my mother for the next eighteen months. She continued to live in her home. When she needed to venture out, either my aunt or a friend of Mom's, Ms. B., whom we compensated, would transport Mom to doctors' appointments, the pharmacist, and the grocery store. Because of the increased flexibility offered by my new assignment and because of a very understanding boss, I also was able to accompany her to various appointments over those months. By combining the information I was getting when I accompanied Mom to an appointment with the information Aunt Millie and Ms. B. were gleaning from the doctors on my mother's behalf, a much clearer and more complete picture of her total health began to emerge.

My learning curve regarding my mother's health challenges during that time was exponential. I learned that with diabetes, especially if the patient struggled to keep their diet in check, raging bladder infections were common, and my mom certainly had her share. I learned that even though she had never smoked a cigarette in her life, she had what the doctor termed as "smoker's lungs." I also learned from him that any bout with pneumonia would likely present a serious threat to her life. I learned from her ophthalmologist that she had macular degeneration and that her sight was affected precisely in the middle of her field of vision.

This explained why I had seen her turn her head a bit to the side when reading something up close—and also likely why she never missed seeing the circus peanuts and the sugared orange slices hovering in her periphery as she walked the aisle of a convenience store.

I remember accompanying her to an appointment with her endocrinologist that turned out to be rather poignant. We were anticipating receiving the results from an internal organ MRI her doctor had recently ordered, and she was slated for blood work for which she had fasted. As we sat side by side in the crowded waiting room, I suddenly noticed her head snap back rigidly and her eyes roll up. The next thing I knew she had fainted and was limp in the chair. I made sure she was lodged securely and bolted for the front desk. Within seconds a team of nurses responded with the doctor's office version of a crash cart and began their work. I reminded them she had not had any food that morning, but of course I had no idea if this was the cause. After just a few minutes, she came around and they offered a little jelly-like substance designed to restore low blood sugar in a controlled manner. The doctor himself came to the waiting room and, upon determining she was stable, asked the nurses to go ahead and take us back.

Once settled in an examining room, the nurse came in to draw the blood sample and asked Mom how she was feeling. My mother said she was feeling better, and in truth she did have her color back. When the doctor came in to examine her, he told us that her blood sugar had been acceptable and that the fainting spell was likely a vasovagal attack, which I later learned was rather common for people of all ages and was just a fancy name for fainting. Far more worrisome, however, was his report that the MRI had detected a fair-sized mass on her pancreas, and he asked us to schedule a followup appointment in three months.

Because of the earlier drama in the waiting room, Mom was gifted with a chariot ride back to the car at the conclusion of his examination; so while I gathered our coats and purses, the nurse wheeled Mom out the office door and into the hallway. Just before I stepped out into the hallway, the receptionist called out to me. "Ms. Collins, the doctor would like to speak with you for a moment." "Certainly," I responded. He joined me in the waiting room, which was oddly empty at that moment, and extended his arm for me to have a seat. He sat down next to me and began to talk. He said, "Mother has a lot going on." I instantly picked up on his choice of phraseology. He had not said, "Your mother has a lot going on." He continued, "I would strongly advise that if Mother ever goes down, you not resuscitate her. I know that's a difficult thing to hear. Also, if she does not have a living will, I advise you to get one." He took my hand and patted it, and through the tumble of thoughts that his words had caused, I thanked him and promised him I would consider his advice on both counts.

On our way home that afternoon, Mom and I discussed the fainting spell, the pancreatic mass and the Living Will. The fainting spell I had witnessed was disturbing for a number of reasons, most obviously another episode occurring while she was standing versus sitting and a serious fall ensuing. We agreed the pancreatic mass just was what it was and we would have to wait a few months to see if it grew in size, Mom adding, "We'll cross that bridge when and if we get there." For the record, we didn't have to cross that particular bridge as the followup MRI three months later showed no increase in the size of the tumor. The easiest of the three subjects was the Living Will, and we decided we both needed one, neither of us wishing to have our life prolonged by any artificial means. I told Mom I would make an appointment with our attorney and have the documents drawn up.

By 2005 the little medicine dispenser that have served Mom well for several months was no longer getting the job done. When I began to find little bins full of pills that had rotated back underneath the solid lid, it signaled me that somehow Mom had failed to take them. I knew the alarm that sounded with each rotation of the circular tray would eventually shut off to protect the battery life; so I reasoned she was either no longer able to hear it or no longer able to recognize what it was telling her. Whatever the case, I lost faith in the little machine as our dispensary.

In retrospect, I had tried many methods to facilitate her continuing to live in her own home, but my doubts regarding the wisdom of that pursuit were mounting. It was becoming clearer by the month that perhaps it was time for me to consider a different place for Mom to live, a safer place, where she would be surrounded by professionals dedicated to the well-being of seniors. Aunt Millie had been somewhat of a godsend, but she had a life of her own, children and grandchildren whom she wanted to spend time with. It was unfair to expect her to forego those opportunities just because it was best for my mother not to be alone for extended periods of time.

When Mom and I discussed the subject of her living somewhere else, she actually seemed quite content with either choice. I, on the other hand, found myself in a daily mental wrangle with the pros and cons offered by each option. Thankfully, as a byproduct of my mental gymnastics, I remembered a Biblical method my mother had taught me decades earlier that could be employed when one needed to make a fork-in-the-road type decision. I had first used it to decide which college to attend and thought it definitely worth a try in this situation. On my next visit with my mother, I offered, "Mom, let's put out the fleece and see which direction God wants us to take." "Okay, baby," she said, "let's do that."

The sixth chapter of the book of Judges in the Old Testament records the story of God and Gideon where God promises to use Gideon to save Israel from several eastern tribes who were punishing the Israelites for disrespecting their eastern god, Baal. At one point, prior to battle, Gideon says to God, "If you will save Israel by my hand as you have promised—look, I will place a wool fleece on the threshing floor. If there is dew only on the fleece and all the ground is dry, then I will know that you will save Israel by my hand, as you said." Verse thirty-eight records that is exactly what happened. When Gideon squeezed the fleece he wrung out a bowlful of dew, yet the ground around the fleece was dry. In true human fashion, Gideon asked permission to test the Lord once more, this time requesting the opposite. The next morning Gideon saw that the fleece was dry and the ground was covered with dew. As a Sunday School teacher, my mother had taught a modern day application for this ancient Biblical story—when one had an important choice to make, prayerfully request that God's will be done and then ask God for a sign. That is precisely what we did.

6

Our sign came in the form of a very short and simple examination by a Birmingham neurologist on October 3, 2005. We had been referred to him by my mother's general practitioner, and I honestly did not know what to expect from the visit. On our drive across town to his office, I noted my mother to be quite peaceful and relaxed, the normal state of the vast majority of our time together as adults. She was predictably very excited about eating breakfast out with me that morning as I had promised. When I pulled my car into the McDonald's parking lot, just a few short blocks from the doctor's office, she looked over at me and grinned.

Over breakfast we talked a little about the upcoming visit, and I learned that she was in the same boat with me, neither of us knowing precisely what to expect. Of course we knew he was a neurologist, and I told her that maybe he could give her some medicines to help her remember things better. She was all for that. I also told her that he might give her some tests to determine how her brain was functioning and then continued, "Mom, like you have always told me, just do your best. That's all a mule can do." We both got a chuckle out of that.

I recall very specific details of Dr. T's examination of my mother that morning, and I remain to this day amazed that such an elementary set of questions could reveal so much. We were shown to an examination room shortly after arriving; just minutes later the medium heighth, red-haired, boyishly handsome doctor came into the room. He was all business, kind enough, but very focused on the task at hand, and after introducing himself, started right in with the questioning. We both gave him our undivided attention. He asked for her name, her birthday, and her Social Security number, all of which she answered correctly and without hesitation. He then asked her what year it was, and when Mom told him that it was 1986, my eyebrows shot up and I mentally braced for what I feared might turn out to be a series of surprises. He asked her what month it was, and she told him, correctly, October. She then gave incorrect answers to his next three questions—the day of the week, the day of the month, and the President of the United States. He then asked her to count backward, starting at one hundred, by sevens. I remember wondering if I could even do that, but my mother didn't miss a beat. She counted, "100, 93, 86, 79, 72, 65." "Okay, okay," he said with a grin. Then he said, "Ms. Collins, I am going to tell you three words that I want you to remember. I am going to distract you for a few moments after I give you the words, and then I am going to ask you to repeat them back to me, okay?" "Okay," she said. "Ms. Collins, the words are *penny, apple,* and *table.*" He then scissored the bottom half of his necktie between the index and middle finger of his right hand and flipped it a little and then asked her what it was. "Tie," she said. "And what is this?" he asked, pulling the writing pen from his pocket and showing it to her. "Pen," she said. "And what is this thing around my neck?" he asked. "Stetch-a-scope" she labored, mispronouncing a word that I knew she was familiar with. No more than sixty seconds had passed since he had given her the three words to remember, and when he asked her to recall them, I held my breath. She hesitated, "Ummmmmmm, cent, ummmmmmm—I don't know." I was equal parts shocked, guilt-ridden, and saddened and wondered if those were akin to her emotions forty years ago when she learned I couldn't see the big E.

At the conclusion of the exam, Dr. T. shared with me matter of factly that she had Alzheimer's disease. He also shared that new research had shown some positive results for slowing the advance of the disease by combining two medicines that had theretofore been given singularly. He prescribed both and told me to ensure she began taking them as soon as possible. He reminded me that Alzheimer's disease was not revertible; one could only hope to slow its pace. He also gave me some literature to help me understand the disease itself and the different symptom-based stages in which it typically manifests.

That diagnosis was indeed the tipping point for our relationship. The moment the word Alzheimer's spilled from Dr. T's mouth, the role reversal that had begun a few years earlier was completed. I was now the de-facto mother and she the child, and I would henceforth manage every detail of her life for as long as she remained on this earth. I was not afraid of that challenge, as I knew she wouldn't be; in fact, I was somewhat relieved to have a clear direction in which to head.

As we drove back to her home that afternoon, Mom and I talked a bit about the appointment, and I gently reminded her that she didn't answer all of his questions correctly. I said, "Mom, you told him the year was 1986." "I did?" she asked, "Well, what year is it?" she continued, giggling a little. I laughed too, likely to keep from crying. I continued, "Mom, I think our fleece just came back wet, and I think we are being led to find you a safer place to live; are you okay with that?" "Yes, honey, whatever you think best," she said. With that, I reached over to hold her hands for a few moments and for the one-thousandth time noticed how soft and warm and beautiful they were.

We slipped back into a companionable silence for the remainder of the long drive. While she stayed in her relaxed and peaceful state, I found myself neither relaxed nor peaceful as my mind raced about, building a to-do list, while my heart lay heavy in my chest, wrapped in a hot, itchy blanket of guilt.

I admonished myself, asking how in the world I had missed such obvious signals. Did I truly fail to recognize them, or did I fail to want to recognize them? I wasn't certain, but whatever the case, I definitely didn't have time to wallow in self-pity. I needed a plan, and I needed to implement that plan post-haste. Thankfully, neither my mother nor anyone else had been harmed during the period of my inaction. I mentally celebrated that fact and saw it as divine intervention, plain and simple. I whispered to myself, "Thank you, Jesus."

The literature Dr. T. had provided was very helpful as it described the seven stages of Alzheimer's in thorough detail. I read every word. Based on his examination, combined with my own experiences with her, it was readily apparent that the disease had advanced well past the first two stages. As I read through the symptoms for Stage 3, I mentally checked them off: mild changes in memory—check; slower reaction time when driving—check; problems producing the right word for objects—check; decrease in planning skills—check; forgetting material that has just been read—check.

I then went down the list of Stage 4 symptoms: forgetful of recent events—check; impaired mathematical ability (for instance, difficulty counting backward from one hundred by nines)—no; forgetful of personal details—no. My mother's flawless execution of counting backward from one hundred by sevens and her ability to remember her name, her birthday, and her Social Security number had served to halt her classification, at least in my mind, at "not yet full-blown Stage 4," i.e., Early Stage-Mild Alzheimer's. I felt strangely better somehow.

The literature also served to paint a vivid picture of the symptoms that would likely manifest over the next few years as she digressed into the more serious stages. My hope was that the drug combination prescribed by Dr. T. would indeed be successful in slowing the advance of the disease; looking back, I judge that it was. Interestingly enough, the two symptoms associated with Alzheimer's that my mother never manifested in the least were the tendency to wander and the significant personality changes, such as being argumentative, impulsive, angry, and combative. In fact, her behavior was just the opposite. She remained sweet, very loving, and submissive to anything we needed for her to do. She was also very respectful of her caregivers, which made them fall in love with her. In spite of the disease, I viewed her behavior over the last six years of her life as a blessing from God. I have often wondered what I would have done had she turned mean-spirited and been hurtful to others. Thankfully, that was never the case. In fact, neither I nor any of our family or friends ever saw the infamous temper again. It was as if the disease had decided that she didn't need that anymore and had just swept it away.

It seemed logical that finding a suitable place for her to live was my top priority and second only to notifying our family and friends. I also believed, correctly as it turned out, that Aunt Millie and Jennifer would not mind lending a hand, watching Mom a little closer short term until I could get things arranged. Figuring out her finances, obtaining power of attorney so I could act on her behalf, and figuring out how we would fund her new living arrangements were running neck-and-neck for third, but would certainly not take a back seat for long. My mother's excellent credit history was another hallmark of her solid-citizen, honest self; and no matter her health challenges, I refused to take chances with it. I concluded that this was basically a multi-pronged advance and I would have to take steps forward in all of those directions simultaneously. I once again said a silent prayer of thanks for the unwanted transfer to Birmingham and for my very understanding supervisor.

It so happened that one of my work mates at the corporate office was married to a lady in the field of Assisted Living. He and his wife spent nearly an hour on the phone with me one afternoon giving much needed advice and direction. The most salient learning was that actually finding a facility was only half the battle; finding an available room within the facility was the real victory and that I shouldn't be surprised if we had to be placed on a waiting list. Armed with that, I began to do my homework and soon found, by the grace of God I have no doubt, an establishment situated in the suburbs of Birmingham only five miles from my house in one direction and five miles from my office in the other. I decided I would call them and ask if they could give me a quick tour during my lunch hour one day soon. The staff was extremely professional, a good sign I thought, and told me to stop by basically any day of my choosing.

I picked a day for which my work obligations after lunch were nil, thinking that I might run a little longer than an hour, told my boss what I would be doing, and asked if I might return late from lunch. As usual, he was very understanding and wished me luck on finding a suitable place.

As soon as I drove onto the access road, I began taking stock of this potential new home for my mother. It was a multi-story, rectangularly shaped building looking out over some urban woods and a small man-made lake. The exterior was a happy yellow color, and the grounds were replete with attractively landscaped sitting areas. The parking lot was large with the flow of traffic well designed and clearly marked. From the angle afforded by the parking lot I could see that the structure was much deeper than I had initially judged. An extended front porch jutted out from the main entrance and was lined with rockers and benches. My tour of the inside of the facility revealed attractive and clean rooms, with ample sunlight ushered in by the large windows and enough square footage to avoid that closed-in feeling. Some of the rooms looked out over a nicely landscaped inner courtyard featuring a paved walkway that encircled the fountain in the center. The kitchen and dining room, which had large windows completely down one side, were on the first floor, along with the residents' mailboxes, the recreation room, the beauty salon, and the nurses' station. And, in what I thought to be a pleasing, non-threatening way, ingress and egress were controlled through the main entrance. The only disconcerting moment of my tour was when my guide pointed out the stout double-doors at the end of a hallway that led to the Advanced Alzheimer's unit. I refused to give any air-time whatsoever to those mental images and returned my attention to the current reality of my mother's condition and the niceties of this facility. After my tour, I spent a few minutes with the administrator, learning more specifics including the process of applying for residency, the length of the waiting list (oddly short she informed me) and the costs. I left that day upbeat, and optimistic; in anticipation this was indeed the place for Mom, I arranged a visit for us the following weekend.

On Friday afternoon, I drove south to fetch my mother and brought her back to Birmingham to spend the weekend with me. The next morning we left my house early so we could enjoy a leisurely breakfast at the nearby McDonald's I had noticed on my earlier visit. I had a feeling that if this assisted living facility became my mother's new residence, then that McDonald's staff would soon know the two of us by name.

Over coffee, egg sandwiches, and hash browns, we chatted about where we were going and why we were going there. I reminded her that if she was not comfortable with what she saw then I would keep looking. As we drove onto the grounds, I noticed her begin to take stock of the facility, just as I had done a week earlier. She dropped her head a little so she could see under the car's sun visor and scanned right and left, taking in the woods and the lake and the picnic tables adjacent to the building. After introductions, the administrator gave us the basic tour. I watched Mom closely, searching her face and body language for clues as to how the place was feeling to her. When we returned to the reception area, I privately asked her if she thought she could be comfortable here and reminded her that I lived just a few miles away and would visit very often. She answered with a sweet and simple yes.

With a glad heart I made sure Mom was comfortably seated in the reception area and stepped into the administrator's office to make application and place Mom's name on the waiting list. After ensuring I understood the rules regarding administering medicines, items which were and were not allowed in her room, and the payment options available, the administrator rose from her desk to shake my hand and gave me a thick packet of information including some pamphlets to further my understanding of the disease that had brought us there. I thanked her for her time and her efforts on our behalf and went to collect my mother who was patiently waiting, taking in the sights and sounds of her potential new residence.

Later that evening with Mom happily settled in the recliner at my suburban home watching television and munching on peanuts, I began to look through the sheaf of papers the administrator had given me. One of the pamphlets contained specific information about things to consider when setting up the resident's room. For instance, a strategically placed mirror on the wall to ensure they continued to get glimpses of themselves throughout the day was important to remind them of their existence in time and space. Also, having a few clocks in the room, especially a large-faced clock hanging in a prominent location, was a good reminder of upcoming events such as breakfast, lunch, and dinner. Photographs of the resident with different family members, especially photos of joyous occasions in which the resident was a participant, were important reminders of their connection to the outside world. All of this made sense to me, and I vowed to make it happen—we just needed a room.

Within weeks we received the hoped-for phone call. The available room was on the second floor, which meant Mom would have to ride an elevator several times a day. Before deciding, she and I made a couple of dry runs up and down the elevator and agreed that she could handle it with relative ease. We then took the necessary steps with the facility's management to secure the room, and I exhaled a little as I mentally struck priority one off the list.

My mother and I received a lot of help from friends and family to accomplish the next important steps. Our lawyer quickly drew up the Power of Attorney, and then my mother's local bank expedited allowing me access to her accounts so I could pay her bills. A friend of mine with a gift for decorating was the creative force behind making my mother's new room beautiful, comfortable, and functional. She also found an appropriate spot for the huge print of a torero, or bullfighter, my mother had purchased from the dollar store years earlier and declared to be "the most beautiful man" she had ever seen. He was a pretty man, decidedly Spanish with his thick beautiful lips, dreamy brown eyes, and jet black wavy hair. He had hung on the wall of her home for years, and I was determined he would be one man who would never leave. Mom's long-time friend Jennifer helped go through Mom's belongings, readying the house for sale, packing things Mom wished to keep, and either selling or giving away the other items. Aunt Millie focused on getting herself packed up and finding another abode while my father took the lead to get the house on the market. The efforts of these friends and family members were helpful beyond description, and I can only hope we expressed our gratitude at the time in appropriate measure.

My mother stayed in the Birmingham assisted living facility for the next two years and by all indications was quite comfortable there. Her thrice daily trek up and down the elevator for her meals had not presented any challenges whatsoever, especially when she used the sturdy wooden walking stick Uncle Gary had gotten for her. As far as her inner-facility social life went, she seemed content and must have been engaged to some extent with the other residents because they voted her their ombudsman. She shared this news with me one day during a visit. I felt extremely proud of her and thought this must be what it feels like when your child is recognized for an award at school. I honestly wasn't sure how the process worked; but I knew an ombudsman was a person who tried to deal with the problems of others fairly, and I thought to myself, "Well, they got the right girl."

I visited at least three times per week and kept her supplied with her favorite brands of lotions, petroleum jelly, dental products, diabetic friendly snacks, and most importantly toilet paper. My mother had always been a fanatic about toilet paper, fastidiously clean; she and I had often joked about how nervous she became if she started to run low on supply. This was just one of her idiosyncrasies, and I thought nothing of it, until the sewage line at my brand new house in Birmingham clogged up one day. Mom had been staying with me, off and on, during our search for her new residence, and I was shocked when the plumber told me the clog was due entirely to an over-abundance of toilet paper. After he unclogged the sewage line and left us that day, Mom and I talked about her hygienic traditions while using the toilet. She apologized for the clog; and I told her not to worry about that at all, but maybe she could modify her technique a little bit. I asked her to demonstrate how she used the paper—the result was a totally mummified right hand, a thumbless white mitten of a thing. I thought to myself with a giggle, "No wonder."

I knew from my reading on the subject of Alzheimer's that engagement was a positive thing, and during the two years she spent in the Birmingham facility, my family and I made sure she was inundated with visitors. Her friend Jennifer, friends from her old church, and my aunts' circle of friends that included Ms. Nita, and my cousin Lynn visited often. Sometimes I would visit her on my lunch hour and eat with her in the facility dining room; sometimes I would bring a friend from work whom Mom did not know and introduce them to her, thereby engaging her socially when meeting someone new. I also decided to keep a decades-old promise that my ex-husband and I had made to each other, that being if anything ever happened to our parents we would notify the other out of respect for the eight and one-half years they had been our respective in-laws.

I cleared the invitation through Mom, ensuring that she in fact remembered him and would like to see him again. She confirmed such; but not being totally sure how long my mom would remember who he was, I focused on finding contact information for him. I had had no contact with my ex-husband in over seventeen years, but I managed to contact him through friends of friends and told him about Mother's diagnosis. He said he appreciated my call and would like to see my mother again. Since his job took him up and down the state several times a year and almost always through Birmingham, he felt that it wouldn't be long before he was in the area again. He promised to call ahead of time and asked specifically that I accompany him on the visit.

It wasn't more than a month before I heard back from him. We set a specific day and time to meet at the facility. As I got out of my car and began walking toward him, I extended my hand in greeting. He took my hand, but instead of shaking it, used it to pull me respectfully into a gentle embrace. I accepted it and viewed it as his wordless way of saying, "I forgive you."

The visit between the three of us was warm and friendly. Mom and I mostly listened as he caught us up on his life. By all indications he was doing very well personally and professionally and my mother and I were indeed happy for him. I was so glad I had listened to my instincts and followed through with making contact. I felt the visit had benefited all three of us.

As I had hoped, following the flurry of activity in the last few months, our lives had fallen back into a comfortable rhythm, reminiscent of years gone by. Every other weekend I would travel to Eufaula to check on my home there and would make sure Aunt Gail knew I would be out of pocket and that any emergency response would be hers to handle initially until I could return to the city. Fortunately, we never had to implement that plan. Occasionally I would take Mom to a restaurant for lunch or dinner. If I could talk her out of a double cheeseburger from McDonald's, then we would go somewhere a little fancier.

During one particular weekend lunch, we were joined by my cousin Trudy at a sit-down chain restaurant near one of Birmingham's large malls. Trudy, the eldest daughter of Uncle W. A., lived about thirty minutes northeast of Birmingham. Mom and I had seen her for the first time in many years at the funeral of her father back in December 2004. She and I exchanged numbers that day and promised to keep in touch.

For two people who were not kin, there were some striking similarities between Trudy and my mother. A large black-and-white portrait of Trudy hanging in my aunt and uncle's living room revealed a very attractive young woman, strongly favoring the black-and-white photos I had seen of my mother at that same age. Both women were decidedly strong, each having eventually landed on her feet after a very hurtful divorce. They were also equally disinclined to take disrespectful treatment from anyone without a challenge; yet they both had hearts of gold and would have gone out of their way to help anyone who needed it.

After we ordered our lunch that day, we enjoyed our iced tea and warm bread and our interesting conversation until our main courses arrived. At one point, about half-way through our meal, my mom had apparently taken a bite of steak that she found too tough to chew and without any hesitation mildly spit it back out onto her plate. Trudy and I locked eyes, and she wordlessly sent me a non-judgmental message of empathy. I reached over and subtly placed a folded paper napkin over the unattractive half-chewed food and gently smiled at my mother. She was worsening, without question, but thankfully it seemed to be at a very slow pace.

By this time, Mom's diabetes was best controlled with measured doses of insulin, and a member of the nursing staff gave her the daily shot, along with a gaggle of pills she took morning, noon, and night. Mom had always had a very active gag reflex; so she countered that by taking the pills one at a time. Her methodology was rote, the variations in it only slight, as she systematically worked her way through the palm-full of meds. She would place one pill on her tongue, drink some water, and then throw her head back rather violently, sweeping the med in a little wave of water that ushered it down before her gag reflex knew what had happened. Consequently, it took a while for her to ingest all of her medicines. The nurses however didn't seem to mind and often shared with me how much they enjoyed their time with her; it was not the least bit unusual for them to approach me while I was visiting her and spontaneously say, "We just love your mother."

For almost two years, our Birmingham base allowed us easy travel to attend family gatherings around the traditional holidays of Easter, Thanksgiving, and Christmas. Also, the first Sunday in May was an Adams family tradition, when as many of us as possible would attend church together and then visit the adjacent cemetery where the departed members of my Adams family are buried. After the visit to the cemetery, we would gather at Aunt Gail's house, just a few miles away, and share a wonderful meal together. For as long as I can remember, this had been a big event and had actually grown over the years to include not only family but dear close friends.

I believed with all of my being that these festive family occasions were healthy outings for my mother; and even though she often appeared distracted, I just knew that on some level she was benefiting from the friendship and love that surrounded her.

What had begun as almost a frantic effort to ensure this new chapter in my mother's life opened smoothly, had transitioned over time into a peaceful, orderly existence. Even though the decision-making dynamic had irreversibly shifted between us, our loving relationship remained unchanged.

7

In early November 2007, I was offered a position back at the nuclear plant near Dothan and was extremely pleased at the thought of returning to the area. The Birmingham assignment had indeed been a godsend; but Mom was relatively stable now, and I was looking forward to once again living in my lake home. The challenge of finding a suitable place for her to live once again took residence at the top of my priority list. Benefiting from the experiences of the last search, I dove into the homework.

There were several facilities available within a sixty-mile radius of Eufaula. Some of the nicer facilities were located in Dothan, a fair-sized city by Alabama standards and at least five times larger than Eufaula. The upside of a Dothan facility was twofold, the closer proximity to my work and the in-house professional nursing staffs. The downside was they were all at least an hour's drive from my home. I thought about the challenges the distance might present, especially in the event of a weekend emergency. There were two facilities in Eufaula proper, both only a few miles from my home, but neither offering a professional nursing staff. The local hospital was only blocks away, which was a plus, but I worried about the daily regimen of pills and the daily shot of insulin that my mother depended on. On one of my every-other-weekend trips to Eufaula, I decided to pay a visit to the larger of the two assisted living facilities and check it out for myself. I found it to be a pleasant, clean, and attractive establishment that offered housing for about twenty residents, a definite upside I thought. It was located near the high school within easy earshot of the football stadium, and I imagined how my mother might enjoy hearing the cheers of the crowd and the band playing during a game. I met with the administrator and talked about my biggest worry, my mother's medications. She was clear to point out that her staff was not licensed to administer meds or to give shots, but they were allowed to assist. I wondered if assistance might be all that she needed and decided it was time to get my mother's input.

After I returned to Birmingham, I made a point of visiting Mom as soon as possible. As we sat in the comfort of her sunny room, I told her of the events that had transpired over the last two weeks. I told her about my new job offer back at the plant and that I would be the first female to ever hold this position within my company. I told her about the facility I had visited—how clean it was, how big the rooms were, and how close it was to my house on the lake. I also mentioned the football stadium nearby and painted a word picture for her of a football game being played there—the crowds cheering, the band playing, and the huge stadium lights burning vividly against an autumn evening sky. She watched me and listened intently. I continued, "Mom, there is one down side. You would have to administer your own insulin shot. Do you think you could learn to do that?"

I knew from her stories about nurse's training in Atlanta in the 1940s that she had learned to give shots by practicing on an orange, and I was hopeful some of that memory was still intact. She appeared to think about the question for a short moment; then with a little nod she answered, "Yes, I think I can do that." I then asked about her feelings regarding the concept of a move in general, away from this nice place. She said, without hesitation, "I want to be near you."

With a sense of relief, I contacted the facility in Eufaula and made application for the two-room, one-bathroom suite that was currently available. I shared with the nursing staff in Birmingham that Mom would soon be leaving their care for another facility in south Alabama near where I lived and worked and that, once there, it would be necessary for her to administer her own insulin injections. They were extremely kind and said they would begin to teach her how to do that. During my next visit just a few days later, with the nurse coaching her, Mom demonstrated her refreshed shot-giving skills for me. She pulled up her blouse, pinched up about two inches of belly fat, and just like that, it was done. The nurse and I cheered and applauded.

For the next several days, Mom stayed in the Birmingham house with me while I packed up her belongings for the move south. I hired a professional moving crew to move her furniture; then Mom and I, as planned, outran the heavy, lumbering truck to Eufaula. I settled her at my lake house and returned to the facility to await the movers and supervise the off-load. Once again, my talented, creative friend was there to provide design advice.

Even though the Eufaula two-room suite was larger than the Birmingham accommodations, we attempted to set it up as similarly as possible to her accustomed arrangement. We placed her bed and dresser in one room; her recliner, her television, and a small library table I had taken out of storage were put in the other room. The library table fitted perfectly underneath the large picture window, and we placed the framed photographs of my mother with family and friends on top of it, all facing her recliner. I also ensured the little ceramic statue of the sad clown she loved had a spot of honor atop the library table. The living room was large enough to accommodate a small couch for guests; so we bought one and moved it in as well. We placed the large-faced clock on the wall near her recliner, and the large mirror from her Birmingham room was on the wall directly above her chest of drawers and along her primary path of travel from one room to the other. The bathroom directly off her bedroom had ample storage space for her toiletries, and I made sure it was well stocked with "you know what." After a few hours of work, everything was ready for her; but believing it was important for her to have uninterrupted adjustment time in her new residence, I decided to push her move-in date back a couple of days, thus allowing us to be in Birmingham for the Thanksgiving holiday. So I returned to the lake house for her and we drove back to Birmingham as planned.

On Thanksgiving Day, after a delicious turkey and dressing dinner with our family and a day of watching football, we returned to my house in the suburbs and spent the night. The next morning I was anxious for Mom to see her new digs; so as soon as we were up and dressed, we set out for Eufaula. We stopped about ten miles down the road to have breakfast, this time choosing a Waffle House. After we ordered, the waitress brought us cups of steaming coffee and I waited for the line that never got old to come from my mother's sweet mouth upon taking her first gentle sip of the black brew she loved—she did not disappoint, sipping and then saying, "Mmmmm, that is so good. I like my coffee, like I like my men, dark and hot." I smiled and laughed and thought to myself how very blessed I was.

It was a pleasant few hours in the car with her and we chatted a little, but mostly we were quiet and reflective. I was thinking about my new assignment and knowing how demanding it had appeared to be for all of my predecessors, worried a little bit about my ability to keep a work/ life balance. My mother was for all intents and purposes my young child, and I had to ensure that her needs were met at any cost. When we pulled into the parking lot of the new facility, Mom began taking stock, just as she had done two years before with the Birmingham place. I chose a parking spot facing the side of the structure so she could continue her perusal and then reached over to unfasten her seatbelt. Before we got out of the car, I pointed out the football stadium and the sign in the front yard of the facility bearing its name, with the little ceramic rabbit someone had placed beneath it. As we walked arm in arm along the short sidewalk connecting the parking lot to the front entrance, she paused briefly a couple of times to take a careful look around. Although it was late November and the air was a bit nippy, the sun was high and bright and made being outdoors more than inviting. As we approached the shaded front porch, I pointed out the swing and the rockers—at the time almost completely full of people relaxing together. Some were obviously residents and the others I guessed were either family or caretakers. I introduced my mother and told them she would be living there, starting today. Smiles and head nods and words of welcome came at us from all directions. My mother smiled too and graciously returned their warm greetings. Thanking everyone on the porch one last time and promising to see them soon, I opened the front door and allowed my mother to go in ahead of me.

The structure itself was a simple single-story laid out in the shape of a large T. Long hallways, containing several suites each, moved off to the right, to the left, and straight back from the centered front porch. The front door opened directly into a well-appointed common area featuring two large front-facing picture windows, plump couches, high-back chairs, polished wood side tables, and a nice piano, which I made a point of showing to my mother. The dining room was straight in front of us, behind a half-wall and featured several tables, some round and some rectangular, with chairs pushed up neatly into place. Nearby was a small busy-sounding kitchen.

The administrator's office was just off to our right, overlooking the common area. When I saw the administrator in her office, I took Mom over to introduce her. She was extremely gracious and took us to meet the small staff, most of whom were in the kitchen clearing away dishes and cleaning up after lunch. As in most southern homes, the kitchen appeared to be the center of life. It contained a normal-sized stove with the requisite aluminum foil-covered left-over pie sitting on the white enamel surface, an oversized refrigerator, and a sink. White countertops connected the sink, the dishwasher, and the stove in an L-shape along two walls. A large walk-in pantry, featuring several shelves replete with canned goods and staples in see-through containers, was built into the opposite wall adjacent to the refrigerator. The staff introduced themselves, drying their hands on a dishtowel before shaking ours. They said comforting words to me such as "Don't worry about your momma" and "We'll take care of her."

After a few more minutes of pleasantries, Mom and I left them to their tasks, thanking them for their hospitality, and walked down the left-hand hallway to her new room. I reached and opened the door to her new suite, swinging it wide and stepping back so she could peer in. I could tell her initial reaction was positive, which made me happy. I began the tour by pointing out her clock, prominently hung adjacent to her recliner, and reminded her of the hours for breakfast, lunch, and dinner. I showed her the remote for her television and gave her a quick refresher on the basics—On/Off, volume control, and channel selection. I pointed to her new couch and told her we had bought it so visitors would have a place to sit (remembering that my ex-husband had to sit on Mom's bed when he visited her). She nodded approvingly. I showed her the phone we had placed on a side table within easy reach of her recliner, made sure my number was programmed as the number 1, and then gave her a quick tutorial on how to reach me. As we stepped into her bedroom, I pointed at her beloved bullfighter, in his *traje de luces,* or "suit of lights," and his *montera* atop his beautiful head of shiny black hair. I imagined he was once a grand oil painting someone had decided to mass-produce and then sell at the dollar store. But regardless of his heritage, his dreamy brown eyes followed you all around the room, and my mother loved him. We had chosen a special place for him, directly on the wall beside her bed. I told her, grinning, "We put him there so he would be that last thing you looked at before you went to sleep." She gave me her broad toothy grin.

The metal-art barn I had bought for her when I was sixteen from a local furniture store hung behind her bed. I knew she wanted it badly back then but couldn't justify spending $150.00 for it. I had an after-school job that year and established a layaway plan with the furniture store. I paid $15 per week for eleven weeks until the bill was paid in full. She was overwhelmed when I brought it home to her, and it had hung on the wall of every home that she had lived in since.

As we checked out her bathroom, I emphatically pointed out the emergency cords and reminded her that she could pull them in an emergency and they would summon one of the staff to come help her. I then opened the vanity cabinets to show her the dozens of rolls of toilet paper stocked inside. Again, she gave me the big toothy grin.

Returning to her bedroom, I opened her closet door and showed her where her outfits were hanging and her shoes were stored. I rounded out her tour by showing her which dresser drawer I had chosen for her socks, her tee shirts (her top body undergarment of choice after the second mastectomy), and her underwear. I told her I had placed the mirror above her chest of drawers so she could see how cute she was everyday—another grin.

She seemed well pleased with her new residence, and I was thrilled with that. I asked her if she wished to go to the common area and visit or to watch television until dinner time. She opted for television; so I left her in her recliner, munching on the dry-roasted peanuts placed within easy reach on her side table. After fetching her a bottle of water from the little fridge we had included as an amenity, I kissed her good afternoon. I told her once again how very proud I was of her and then left, closing the door behind me.

On my way out, I stopped by the office and told the administrator that Mom was settled and asked that they kindly remind her of the dinner hour until she got into a routine. They promised that if she didn't show up for any meal they would indeed be checking on her. My final stop was the medicine room, no bigger than a closet nestled into a space right behind the dining room and which remained locked at all times unless a staff member was inside. I performed a final review of her list of medicines with the staff member assigned to that task and ensured they remembered she would need assistance with her insulin shot. I then left, feeling comfortable, and drove the few miles to my home overlooking the lake.

Later that evening, I made one last "I love you" and "sleep tight, don't let the bedbugs bite" phone call to my Mom's room. I felt assured that all had gone well on her first day in this new place, and I thought to myself, "Thank the Good Lord, so far, so good."

The next three weeks passed uneventfully. My new job was proving to be every bit as challenging as I thought it would be, but I was truly enjoying being back in the thick of things.

Mom was faring well and was, as I had suspected would soon happen, making new friends and admirers, the staff never missing an opportunity to tell me how much they were enjoying her. At least half of the staff at the new facility were of African-American descent, and I can only surmise that trying to help Caucasian people of my mother's generation could at times be challenging, especially in the Deep South and especially if the residents' good manners had gone by the wayside along with their mental acuity. When someone like my mother came along, someone who had never seen color and didn't see it now, she was bound to stand out as a unique and loving human being. I believed the staff sensed her genuine love and appreciation for every little thing they did for her, and my mother's behavior once again made me feel like a proud parent.

The Birmingham home had been on the market for only a few weeks and had not yet sold. So I decided that over the upcoming Christmas holidays Mom and I would use it as a home base while we joined our family and friends for the traditional gatherings on Christmas Eve and Christmas Day.

For most of my life, my parents and I had spent Christmas Eve at Aunt Gail's home in Hoover. It was always a grand affair. My aunt would have her entire house tastefully decorated, usually including a beautiful sparkling pristine white tree upstairs and a more traditionally decorated green tree downstairs; my uncle would lay a fire in the downstairs fireplace giving the whole house a hint of the comforting wood smoke smell. My family knew the real reason for the season, all having grown up in the Christian faith; so among the more glitzy decor, my aunt always found a prominent place to display her beautiful ceramic nativity scene.

The Adams family had no shortage of excellent cooks, and our tradition was to eat finger foods on the night before Christmas and save our sit-down grand meal for Christmas Day. My aunt had often spoken of Christmas as her favorite holiday, and her efforts to show her family how much she loved us was never in stronger evidence than on those two days.

It is my belief that after my grandmother passed away in 1993, a sliver of the joy my aunt felt for the holiday had died with her. They had, after all, lived together for my aunt's entire life, and their mother-daughter relationship was akin to the special bond I shared with my own mother. But at some point during the fourteen years that had elapsed since my grandmother's death, a shift had occurred in our family dynamic; we had spent the last few Christmas Eves at Uncle Bill's house in Adamsville, Alabama, a short drive northwest of Birmingham. My mother adored her brother, and had looked out for him as only a big sister could when they were younger. She easily looked past his personality traits that caused me to dislike him—I loved him, but did not like him. I considered him a classic bully. I had witnessed him bullying his daughter, my precious cousin Donna, years ago when we were both children, embarrassing her unnecessarily in front of me and her friends, and had never forgotten it.

On this particular Christmas Eve, my uncle was ensconced in his favorite recliner doing his favorite thing, watching football with some of the menfolk, while the rest of the family milled about visiting, talking, and snacking. The young people were playing games together, or just visiting in various parts of the big house, the very youngest of them wondering how Santa was faring. Uncle Bill had not been well of late and, like my mother, had a weakness for food that was not beneficial to his health, sometimes even detrimental. My mother and I were purposely sitting close to him so that she could converse with him during football timeouts and commercial breaks. Watching them talk, glancing back and forth between them, I would get occasional glimpses of their profiles and noted yet again the remarkable similarities in their faces. My cousin Donna and I had talked about that a few times of late and marveled that the older the sister and brother became, the more they looked alike.

My uncle was three and one-half years younger than my mother but didn't really look any younger. I silently looked him over while he volleyed back and forth between watching the game and talking with my mother. He was thinner than I had ever remembered seeing him, his prominent cheeks sunken and peppered with gray stubble, his hair thin and wispy and combed straight back. He was dressed in a flannel shirt and jeans, but no socks nor shoes. While reclined with his legs stretched out, he would sometimes absentmindedly rub the sole of one foot across the top of the other, the sound it made like that of sandpaper on a board.

I do not know to this day what possessed me, but I took yet another page from my mother's book—this one on how kindness should not be predicated upon fondness—and asked Uncle Bill if he would like for me to put some lotion on his feet. He looked at me and smiled—it was my mother's smile—and said, "Yes, Cheri-Pot, that would be great." Cheri-Pot, or sometimes just Pot, had been his nickname for me for as long as I could remember. I asked Aunt Wilma if she would kindly point me in the direction of some lotion. She told me there was a bottle of witch hazel in their bathroom, so I fetched it. I had never heard of witch hazel being used to treat dry skin, but, we live and we learn.

It is noteworthy to point out that I am one of those people who believe that God's intention for the foot was purely utilitarian. I can count on one hand the pairs of feet I have seen in my lifetime that I thought were attractive. My mother's feet were not the least bit symmetrical nor attractive; but they were always very soft, with healthy pink nails always trimmed and clean. My uncle's feet reminded me of my father's feet and were indescribably ugly. The dryness had sketched gray-white lines resembling a road map on both soles; and each craggy toe was topped with a thick, misshaped, discolored, jaggedly-trimmed toenail. I poured the witch hazel into my palm and began massaging his feet. When his oldest granddaughter walked by a few minutes later and saw me rubbing her Paw's feet, she exclaimed, "Ooooo, Cheri, what are you doing? Grooossss!" I smiled, shook my head from side to side as if to answer her question, and then looked over at my mother. She had been watching me and smiled back. I could tell she was very grateful for this small act of kindness toward her declining, beloved brother.

After our Christmas Eve visit at Uncle Bill's house, Mom and I drove to my Birmingham house and settled in for the evening. The moderate brick home in the suburbs that I had lived in for nearly four years had proven to be just what I needed it to be. Large enough, but not too large, certainly comfortable, and with a fenced-in yard and doggie door for my miniature schnauzer Stevie to use, it had met all of my needs. It was a three-bedroom, two-bath arrangement, with the master bedroom and bath on one side of the house separated from the other two rooms and the second bathroom by a large open living room, kitchen, and small eating area. I put Mom in the only guest bedroom that actually had a bed and kept the light on in the bathroom so that she could see more easily if she needed to use the facilities during the night.

In the wee hours of Christmas morning, I was awakened by a distressed sounding call of my name. I was initially confused, in that deep state of sleep thinking that I was dreaming, but the persistent calling out finally worked its way forward into my consciousness and woke me. I realized it was my mother. I flew out of bed and ran across the cold living room floor to her bedroom. The dim light illuminated the figure of my mother lying S-shaped, on the beige carpeted floor at the foot of the bed, cane broken in half beside her. I turned on the bedside table lamp and bent down to her, noting the look of agony on her face. I stroked her cheek and started questioning her as to how she felt: did she think she could sit up? did I need to call 911? She said she thought she had broken something, so I immediately made the 911 summons. While we waited, I laid a small couch throw over her shivering body, told her to lie still, and quickly went to get dressed and put on just enough make-up to be respectable. When I came back, I sat down on the floor with her and just talked to her. I noted the tee shirt and panties she was wearing looked as if they had been Christmas dinner for a horde of moths. I knew she owned much newer undergarments but, like me, just preferred the old, worn-out ones. I gently teased her about the possibility that these paramedics would be quite handsome and were going to see her in those. She grinned through her pain.

As if on cue, the doorbell rang and I went to answer it. Just like in the movies, three handsome, well-built paramedics came into the house and I showed them to the small bedroom where Mom was lying. I told them she feared she had broken something, and then quietly told the lead medic that she had Alzheimer's. They talked amongst themselves trying to figure out how to extract her. The bedroom was small and the bed itself only a few feet from the wall, and the angle of the door with respect to the foot of the bed was quite sharp. They understandably wanted to put her on a backboard, but there was simply not enough space without tilting it at an unreasonable angle, especially if she were strapped to it. I am certain they were only seconds away from thinking the same thing, but suddenly I had a flash of Mom's rescue plan for the large wheelchair-bound boy on her bus. I told them, "I have a blanket in the other room. Could we get it under her and then snake her through the door, out into the kitchen?" "Yes," they said almost in unison. So that's what we did.

They loaded Mom into the ambulance and told me the name of the hospital where they were taking her. I grabbed my purse and car keys and followed them, making a mental point of locking the front door behind me. About ten minutes later, I arrived at the hospital and saw the paramedics off-loading Mom at the emergency room door and the E-room nurses taking over from there. I followed them in. They promised they would come get me as soon as they could, so I took care of paperwork at the admissions desk while they situated Mom in a room. By the time they allowed me to go back to her, they had already taken x-rays and she was in a hospital gown resting more comfortably. While we waited on the doctor, we talked a little bit about what had happened. She remembered using her cane to walk around the edge of the bed on her way to the bathroom, but not much else. I had seen the thick cane broken into jagged halves lying on the floor near her and could only guess she had accidentally placed it between the vertical bars of the metal footboard and then, unable to dislodge it, fell against it with her forward momentum, snapping it in half, losing her balance in the process and landing on her hip.

Soon the doctor came in to see us, and I crossed my fingers that just maybe we were not dealing with a break. But that was not the case, and the surgeon told me that she had indeed broken her hip and that he would like to operate immediately. I, of course, gave consent. While they were prepping Mom for surgery, I spent several minutes with the surgery nurse telling her about Mom's conditions and medicines. She then handed me off to another nurse who showed me to an empty and silent waiting room.

It was early Christmas morning and for the first time in several hours, I had time to actually think and not just react. The quiet waiting room, completely devoid of humans, was the perfect place for pondering the question, "What to do next?" By the grace of God, the on-call doctor for the Christmas holidays was, by reputation, the finest orthopedic surgeon in Birmingham. I sent a silent prayer of thanks, and asked for His abiding presence with my mother, and then tacked on a postscript asking that He give me guidance and that His will be done on all accounts. The words of my mother's endocrinologist echoed in my thoughts, "Mother has a lot going on . . . I recommend that you not resuscitate her." I knew my mother to be at peace with the outcome of this surgery come what may, and in her honor I chose to be at peace as well.

The surgeon had told me when to expect to hear back from him; within minutes of his predictions, he appeared in the door of my waiting room with the good news that Mom had made it through surgery fine. She would be in recovery for about an hour or so, and then I could see her. When I entered her room, she looked over at me and smiled. She was in good spirits, a minor amount of pain but good spirits all the same.

I was incredulous when the attending nurse told me the doctor wanted to get her up within twenty-four hours, walking on the new hip. It was a difficult process for my mother, but she showed her characteristic grit and did as they instructed. The surgeon's goal was clear from the outset. He expected my mother to walk again just as good as she had prior to the break. His office provided information that there were at least three phases of physical therapy to achieve that outcome. The first two were increasingly challenging over time, with the third phase designed as maintenance that would gradually restore her to full walking health.

Fortunately for us, Dothan, Alabama, was home to a fine medical community—two first-rate hospitals, pain management clinics, and state-of-the-art physical therapy facilities. I made arrangements for her to begin her first phase of recovery therapy at a facility in Dothan just one block from the main hospital. She was transported from the Birmingham hospital to the Dothan physical therapy facility (about two hundred miles) via ambulance, running silent. Knowing I would be several hours behind the ambulance, I asked my dear friends Molly and Neecie to intercept her for me. They both lived in the Dothan area, and there were no two people on earth I trusted more. Mom knew them well also, but more by their monikers "Double-Dern" and "Cha-ching"—these nicknames deriving from a fun-filled weekend the four of us had spent together at the Philadelphia, Mississippi, casino several years before.

My mother spent a relatively successful three weeks undergoing physical therapy in this first clinic. I stopped by to see Mom every day after work and my dear friends sprinkled in visits as well. At the end of the first phase of therapy, Mom was transferred to another facility to continue her recovery. This one was located near the city center of Dothan; and again, between my dear friends and me, we made sure my mom saw a familiar face every day. It was in this second facility that I had to deliver the news that Uncle Bill had passed away. I remember my mother's face, tearless but contorted by sadness. When I finished speaking, she looked away from me and off into space, wrapping her mind around the news, and softly spoke the words, "Ohhh, Billy has died." The authenticity of her emotions caused me to choke up and I thought back to Christmas Eve, the smell of witch hazel, his granddaughter's incredulity, and the feel of Uncle Bill's feet in my hands. My mother was right; you never regret an act of kindness.

In the middle of February a couple of weeks before my mother's eighty-first birthday, she returned to her home at the Eufaula assisted living facility. She was using a walker now, and I had learned the trick of putting tennis balls on the tips of the straight legs. When she walked through the front door, the staff greeted her with big smiles and made her feel very welcome. They told her they had missed her and were so glad she was back. I could not have asked for a more perfect homecoming for her.

A lot had changed in those last two months. Although Mom did well with her therapy, upon her release she was not at a point where she could get dressed, use the bathroom, or bathe without assistance. I had come to this conclusion early enough during her weeks of therapy to have time to find, interview, and hire three local women to provide around-the-clock help for my mother. I had also purchased a new recliner for her to use, a motorized one that would slowly assist her from sitting to standing and vice versa with the touch of a button.

I had asked the three caretakers to meet us at the facility on the day of Mom's return so that I could introduce them to her. They had all been recommended to me, albeit in varying degrees: one was said to be "great," one was said to be "good," and the other was said to be "fine." I wasn't sure how long I would need them; but I speculated at least two months; so I drew up a shift schedule taking into account their other commitments and made arrangements to pay them at the end of each week. My mother seemed to be comfortable with all three of the women. Even though I was coming to the realization that my mother was slowly losing her ability to discern, there were other signs that I watched for to ensure that my mother was being taken care of properly. One of the women was a smoker, and although she would always step outside to smoke, my mother's room had a faint odor of tobacco after a period of time with this sitter. She was also heavy and short-legged and typically sat on the very edge of the little couch—I suppose to facilitate her getting up and out of it. Within a month, the cushion refused to return to its normal shape and stayed scooped with the imprint of her rear-end. Over time I thought of one of the sitters as a bit on the lazy side; but again my mother seemed to be faring well, so I kept her on. Ms. Fine and Ms. Good didn't care much for one another and were both simply jealous of Ms. Great. Consequently, on payday, I could always expect to hear a critique of the other two sitters.

But as I knew my mother would want me to do, I just listened—my mother's training echoing in my mind—"listening to others is like giving them a gift."

Ms. Good was very experienced having sat for many residents in her day and preferred the night shift. That fact alone made her invaluable to us, but she was also very responsible and I knew I could trust her to do the right thing for my mom. She recommended I buy a small notebook that each sitter could use to record the events on her shift. This way, she told me, I would have a record of how my mother was doing. I took her advice and soon began to wonder if it had not been just a tinge self-serving, because Ms. Good enjoyed writing in the journal and would write page after page describing the intricacies of the last eight hours with my mother. It took me a while to read through the tightly packed, right-tilted script. Sometimes the information was fascinating, but mostly it was quite ordinary. Ms. Good noted that Ms. Fine could manage to write only a line or two in her eight hours and would typically point that out to me.

Ms. Great came as billed, a sweet-spirited, gentle, and very responsible woman. She was a lovely African-American lady, a wife and mother of four boys, and never had an unkind word to say about anyone. She and my mother soon fell in love, and it was a joy for me to be together with them. Ms. Great's name was Carol. She always referred to my mother as Miss Collins and called me "Shar-ree." She had a lovely voice and conversed in singsong, always seeming to place her words atop a soft bed of laughter. Like my mother, when she got tickled at something she simply gave herself up to it, creating a contagion of laughter affecting anyone else in earshot. After my mother improved to the point it was no longer necessary for twenty-four-hour care, Carol stayed on with us and would spend a few hours in the morning helping my mom get the day started and a few hours in the evening helping her get ready for bed.

Fittingly, I thought, Carol was the person in the hospital room with my mother when she drew her last breath on May 13, 2010. They had become fast friends and had shared great times in the two years they had known each other. Even with my mother's declining mental acuity, she and Carol shared a love and a respect that typically take a lifetime to build. Some of my favorite stories of my mother are those that were relayed to me by Carol.

To celebrate my mother's eighty-first birthday, February 27, 2008, Aunt Gail gathered up as many of the "girls" as she could and made the drive to Eufaula. The girls brought gifts and decorations and food and set up a birthday celebration in the dining hall. Carol joined us for the festivities, and I proudly introduced her to my family and friends. As was typical for this group, everyone was talking and laughing and no one was really listening to anyone else. It didn't matter though, their kindness and their loving spirits had filled Mom's heart with joy, and that was a very good thing.

Aunt Wilma had accompanied them, still grieving the death of her husband, Uncle Bill, just two weeks earlier. For all of his characteristics that I found disappointing, he must have been a very good husband because my aunt adored him. I recognized the sadness associated with loss in her eyes, remembering the time I had seen it twenty-six years earlier when her son Steve had been killed. Only eight months would go by before I would have to deliver the news to my mother that Aunt Wilma had passed away. This, of course, caused her to ask about Uncle Bill, and once again I told her of his demise eight months before. As my friend Neecie had so eloquently put it, the saddest thing about a failing memory was the inevitability of having to feel loss over and over again.

The girls made the drive to Eufaula two more times, celebrating my mother's eighty-second and eighty-third birthdays in the dining room of her assisted living facility, which they always transformed into a party place complete with balloons and cake and gifts. Her beloved sitter, Carol, had been embraced by my family and was always in attendance.

Over the next two years, my life with my mother was a time of great enjoyment. Perhaps that sounds odd given her circumstances, but I had been trained by my mother to understand that we were not designed to be on this earth forever, and in the words of her favorite hymn, "Whatever my lot, Thou has taught me to say, 'it is well, it is well, with my soul.' "

Every weekend we would spend significant time together. Usually I would take her for a drive, somewhere new that offered mental stimulation, giving her a break from her daily routine. Sometimes we would drive out to the lake and I would park the car facing it; and we would sit quietly side by side looking out over the expanse of sparkling water, and I would point out boats and birds and children playing at the river's edge. Sometimes we would just drive through town, south on Eufaula Avenue, which was lovely, shaded under a canopy of oaks and lined on both sides with hundred-year-old southern mansions. Our dialogue on this particular drive became highly predictable—turtling her head slightly down into her neck and looking out the windshield below the sun visor, she would always ask me, "Is this Eufaula?" "Yes, ma'am, it is," I would reply. "The clouds sure are pretty," she would say. "Yes, ma'am, they are," I would respond.

Sometimes we would go out for barbecue at Phil's, just a mile or so away. Their sauce was mustard-based and slightly different from the ketchup-based sauces we were used to, but delicious nonetheless, and we both loved to eat there. One day, as we were headed for lunch at another of her favorite Eufaula spots, The Cajun Corner, which featured delicious fried shrimp, we drove directly past the barbecue restaurant. She pointed over at Phil's and said, "I told him to buy that restaurant." "You did?" I asked playfully, thinking to myself that this was indeed new dialogue territory. She continued, "Yes, he was selling his barbecue out of his house, and I told him if he would buy that building, he would do really well." I responded, "Well, it is a good thing he listened to you, isn't it, Momma?" "Yes," she replied. I glanced over at her and smiled at the humble expression my compliment had put on her face.

On another weekend drive together, she spontaneously offered that she used to play the ukulele and the slide guitar and then said, "And pretty well, I might add." I knew she picked a little guitar in her day but was never very accomplished, and I neither saw nor heard of a ukulele in her repertoire. My father did own and play a slide guitar when I was a small child, so I thought maybe that was the origin for such a memory. I marveled that even though her mental accuracy was in question, her creativity seemed unaffected.

In my new capacity at the nuclear plant, I was blessed to have a magnificent administrative assistant who not only looked out for me professionally, keeping me on schedule and helping me be ready for the next meeting and the next and the next, but also understood my personal life and the responsibilities that came along with caring for my mother. One morning I saw Mary's pretty face peek around the corner of my office door. Mary said, "Carol's on the phone; it isn't an emergency; she just needs to speak with you." I thanked her and took the call.

I heard Carol's beautiful melodic voice on the other end of the phone say, "Shar-ree, honey, yo' momma won't bathe." I responded, "Do tell, Carol." She continued, "Well, I tried to talk her into it, but she just don't want to; I told her, 'Now Miss Collins, you know you have to bathe, especially we have to wash Little Miss Collins.'" (Little Miss Collins was the name Carol had given my mother's private parts, and it never failed to tickle me when I heard her use the nickname.) She continued, "I told her, I said, 'I guess I'm gonna' have to call Shar-ree!'" Then Carol gave me Mom's answer to that threat: "And yo' momma said, 'Call her,'" using the same impish little tone my mother had used as if to say, "See if I care." Both of us giggling at the story, I asked Carol to put Mom on the phone. "Hello," she said. "Hi, Mom, how are you doing?" I asked. "Fine," she said. I continued, "So, Kakki, Carol says you don't want to bathe?" "No," she said. I was completely used to these monosyllabic answers as they had been a feature of my mother's communications for the last few years. She had taught me as a youngster, "Let your *yes* be *yes* and your *no* be *no*," and that there was really no need for embellishment of these two words—it appeared to me that she had never forgotten that advice. I went on, "But, sweetie, you know you have to bathe; you don't want to smell bad, do you?" "No," she said, all of her earlier bravado gone. "Okay, so the next time Ms. Carol says it's time to bathe, what are you going to say?" I asked. "Let's go," she said happily. I grinned from ear to ear and said, "That's my girl, I love you, Momma." "I love you, too," she said; and then Carol was back on the line. We laughed a little together, and I told her I was glad she had called and hoped we had that little issue resolved.

Although my mother was extraordinarily easy to deal with and very sweet, she did have a mischievous streak that would show itself from time to time. One afternoon Carol and I were visiting together in Mom's living room while my mother was hanging out on the toilet. Even though I had purchased a thick plastic seat extension with handles on each side to aid her, it was still an effort for her to get up and down, so once seated she tended to stay there for several minutes, determined to make the trip worthwhile.

Carol had waited for Mom to ensconce herself in the bathroom out of earshot before looking at me, baring her beautiful white teeth in a huge grin, and saying quietly, "Shar-ree, you are not gonna' believe what Miss Collins said to Ms. Crazy." Ms. Crazy was our code name for the lady who lived in a nearby suite. She was suffering from some form of mental decline, but unlike the other residents, she was not yet a widow. Her husband was of sound mind and still lived on his own, and she was quite jealous of him. Carol told me that he had visited that day and left shortly before lunch. She continued, "Shar-ree, Miss Collins and Ms. Crazy are sittin' at the dinner table across from each other and Ms. Crazy looks at yo' momma and says, 'You've been datin' my husband, haven't you?' and Miss Collins said, 'Yeh-es.'" At this, Carol gave in to the laughter she had been holding at bay just long enough to tell the story. I joined her, throwing my head back and then bending forward, slapping my thighs. She went on, "An' then Ms. Crazy said, 'And you're pregnant with his baby, aren't you?' and Miss Collins said, 'Yeh-es.'" With this final punchline, I lost total control, tickled to the point I couldn't utter an intelligible word, wheezing like a car engine trying to start on an empty gas tank. Carol, who had been sitting on the couch during her story, now rolled back into its depth, pulling her knees up to her chest and guffawing in her pure, sweet high voice. Little drops of water squeezed from our slitted eyes, and I dabbed at mine with a knuckle, while Carol removed her glasses and wiped hers away with a tissue from the box on Mom's side table. The next sound we became aware of was the toilet flushing, so we both focused on bringing ourselves back under control before Mom reappeared. As hilarious as this story was, Carol and I were in agreement that it was likely not in Mom's best interest to tease the neighbor about her husband. I heard the familiar *schckk, schckk* of her walker, and soon she made her way into the living room where Carol and I were doing our best to recover. She made her way to her recliner, which was in the upright dump position, leaned back against it, and pressed the button to slowly lower herself to a seated position. As the recliner motor quietly whirred, I was finally able to manage, "Mom, I hear you teased your neighbor today about dating her husband, and maybe being pregnant with his baby?" She looked down at the floor and grinned. I went on, "Now, Kakki, you can't be teasing her about that, sweetie. She's not real stable. She's liable to get a pair of scissors and come in here and take you out!" I knew I was being a bit melodramatic, but I needed to impress upon her the potential seriousness of teasing a jealous woman about her man. She nodded her head in understanding; and as far as I know, she never went down that road again.

On nice sunny weekends I would occasionally take Mom to my lake house. We did this only a few times as it was labored effort for her to climb the three brick steps to the front porch, always having to pause for a moment afterward, leaning on her walker, regaining her breath before continuing into the house. She loved to sit on the deck underneath the big red umbrella shading the teak table and stare out at the water. I would usually fix us a light lunch and we would eat out there together. While I was preparing our food, I would keep an eye on her through the huge kitchen picture window that looked out over the lake to the pine covered hills of Georgia, only a mile away by boat. The sight of her little gray head above the back of the wooden deck chair, held very still while she tranquilly watched the water, made me feel peaceful and happy. I toyed with the idea of taking her on a boat ride, but the steep slope to the water and the challenge and risks associated with actually getting her in and out of the boat caused me to dismiss it, even though I knew she would have enjoyed it.

I noticed over the last twelve months or so of my mother's life that she was becoming less able to fully explain any discomfort she might be feeling. It was as if she knew she was either in pain or discomfort but couldn't pinpoint it or tell me why. Carol and I learned to look for signs that she was in discomfort, such as facial contortions and grunts of anguish when she made certain moves. It became apparent to us that her low back was giving her trouble; so I decided to consult a pain management specialist in Dothan. He told us there was an option for deep, localized injections of steroid and pain reliever made under local anesthesia that would likely provide temporary relief. He had confirmed the presence of a significant amount of arthritis in her low back through x-rays, which came as no surprise to me. I asked about the amount of discomfort she would be in while undergoing the procedure, and he assured me it would be manageable. My mother took three of these injections over several months, and as predicted they became less and less effective over time. The downside of even the partial pain relief was the spike in her blood sugar cause by the steroids. After her third injection, I tried to determine by talking with her if they were indeed worth it to her. I never got a straight answer and truly didn't expect one. But when I talked about a future injection in about three months' time, her face grimaced a little, and I decided then and there, no more.

Her failing ability to explain how she felt or what was causing her to do certain things was never in stronger evidence than the day Carol called me at work and told me Mom wouldn't eat. I couldn't have been more surprised if she had told me my mother had sprouted wings and was flying around the room. Carol and I both knew this was highly unusual. She didn't appear to be sick, no nausea, no stomach pains or cramping, she just wouldn't eat. That morning at breakfast, coffee was the only thing she could apparently stomach. Carol questioned her gently, asking what was wrong and suggesting a bite of eggs or a nibble of toast, but my mother was simply not interested. I thanked Carol for the call and told her I would pick up the gentle interrogation after work and see if I could figure it out.

As Mom and I sat together in her room that afternoon, I picked up where Carol had left off. I asked, "Mom, are you not hungry, sweetie?" "No," she said. I continued, bringing out the big guns, "How about I make you a peanut butter and jelly sandwich?" I saw a flicker of temptation cross her face; then she frowned a painful little frown, and with the smallest little gagging sound said, "Ohhhhh, no, I don't want anything." After continued coaxing, I was finally able to get her to drink some water and eat a few of the dry-roasted peanuts that were always readily available in a jar next to her recliner. In minor frustration, I decided to talk with the staff and left Mom watching a video of one of her all-time favorite entertainers, "Tina Turner, Live from Rio."

(My mother loved Tina Turner and had read her autobiography years ago and thought her to be very strong, able to overcome "Ike's meanness" and quite beautiful, benefiting from the vibrant mix of her heritage, roughly 2/3 African-American, 1/3 European, and about 1%

Native American. Mom also thought she had "the prettiest legs God ever gave a woman." Ms. Turner actually performed in Atlanta on November 9 and 10, 2008, as part of her 50th Anniversary Tour. As the performance dates approached, rumor had it, and the Atlanta disc jockeys confirmed it, there were two tickets available on the front row at the Philips Arena for $2500.00 apiece. If my mother had been more mobile and little stronger, I would have floated a loan if need be to get my hands on those tickets.)

Going to the common area, I found five of the staff members resting together at one of the dining tables, chit-chatting amongst themselves. I pulled up a chair and sat down, asking them to please excuse my interruption, which they did quite graciously. Now having their undivided attention, I explained what was going on with my mother and asked if they knew of anything that had occurred that might have caused my mother to go off her feed. They all watched me while I spoke, listening intently, and then tilted their chins up slightly, looking off into space, searching their memories for a clue. Then they began looking into each others eyes continuing their mental search, lips twisted in thought. After a few minutes of speculating on this cause or that reason, one lady finally said, with an air of excited discovery, "You know, I think Ms. Collins was in the dining hall when we found that smashed fly on the bottom of that pizza we ordered for our lunch yesterday." The others began nodding their heads and I listened as they talked over each other—"Yeap, I think yur right"; "She sure wuz"; "I bet that's it!" Well, I knew her—and I knew that was it.

My mother's eyes and nose had always been hardwired to her appetite. The smell of hot buttered popcorn at the theatre, or the sight of golden fried shrimp on a television commercial, or chocolate cake in a bakery window would cause her to crave it. Conversely, though, the sight or smell of something disgusting would place her highly suggestible gag reflex front and center in her mind. I remembered the story of her and Daddy sharing a can of black-eyed peas together, back before I was born. Apparently they were so hungry they hadn't even bothered to heat them up and were just sharing from the can, one spoonful at a time—until they got to the bottom where they caught sight of half of a small worm—then they shared the toilet, vomiting in turns, pushing the other's head away when one of them couldn't hold back any longer. She never ate anything straight out of a can again. Then there was the sixty-year-old story of the worm she saw inside the peanut butter cup she had just bitten into; he was at least whole, but she swore off peanut butter cups for years afterward.

Believing I finally understood the reason behind her fasting, I thanked the ladies and returned to Mom's room. I really did not know if she remembered the details of the nauseating sight or if she had simply seen something nauseating. I opted to be blunt and just deal with the consequences, hoping that facing it and talking about it would give her some perspective. I said, "Momma, did you see a dead fly on the bottom of the ladies' pizza yesterday?" I watched as a pained expression developed on her face and heard her gag a little and say, "Yes." Okay, I thought, now I have something concrete to deal with. I went on to explain that the ladies had ordered that pizza for their lunch, not hers, it had come from an outside store, and they had not eaten it but had thrown it away. I told her that the food prepared here was not going to have flies on it. We stared straight into each others eyes during my entire explanation. I don't know if it was trust or hunger or a combination of the two that finally won her over, but the next morning Carol called me and said, "We back to normal this morning, Shar-ree; what did you find out?" I told Carol the whole story. She said, "Oh Law, Shar-ree, that would'a got me too!" laughing her pure, sweet laugh.

My mother's inability to quickly shake off disturbing images was not limited to food-related incidents. I knew from her own story that she had brooded for years over the details she overheard of the particularly heinous crime against the young Birmingham boy kidnapped in the 1950s. I also knew that she refused to watch the actor Karl Malden in a film or a television show because she had seen him play the part of a Southern lecher in the 1956 film *Baby Doll*, and in her mind he was permanently typecast. My awareness of this aspect of her personality caused me to try over the years to screen films and television shows in advance of her seeing them, knowing full well that if the subject matter featured deviant behavior or depravity, it would undoubtedly affect her in a most negative way.

In late 1993, the film *Schindler's List* was released to rave reviews and went on to win seven Oscars for its portrayal of the true story of Oskar Schindler, an egotistical and greedy German businessman who became an unlikely humanitarian against the backdrop of Nazi Germany. My mother had heard the positive press on director Steven Spielberg's ingenious and artistic handling of this magnificent story, juxtaposed with the atrocities of, arguably, one of the saddest periods in human history, and was, to say the least, intrigued.

As a long-time Christian, she had read and re-read the Old Testament story of God's chosen people. She had studied in detail the relationship between the Jews and the God of their father Abraham and understood it to be a cycle of human behaviors that they had repeated time after time throughout their history. The cycle always began with obedience, sacrifice, and worship; and then it ran the course through complacency, unfaithfulness, arrogance, remorse, and repentance before finally circling back, through God's unfailing love, to obedience, sacrifice and worship yet again. She had taught me that the spiritual cycle of the Jews was partially replicated in the life of a Christian, different in that Christ was the ultimate sacrifice for our sins and through His death and resurrection we had been given the gift of grace. She believed wholeheartedly in the inextricability of Judaism and Christianity, and she thought that when Christ returned, the Jews and only the Jews would be given a second chance to accept Him as the Messiah. She further believed that the United States had an obligation to never turn its back on the Nation of Israel; and if we ever did, it would be at our own peril.

She and I discussed her desire to throw caution to the wind and see the film. I asked her to please allow me to see it first. She agreed. I sat spellbound in my theater seat for the three-plus hours of film, experiencing a full range of emotions, beginning with incredulity over a civilized nation's ability to somehow justify pervasive inhumanity and ending with admiration and intense sympathy for a man who could no longer look the other way, but was trapped inside an insidiously evil system that allowed him only enough agonizing wiggle-room to save a relative few. There were several scenes that I believed my mother might never be able to erase from her memory, and I strongly advised her not to see the movie. To the best of my knowledge, she never did.

In December 2009, I was offered the opportunity to become a spokesperson for my company's new nuclear reactor projects under construction in Augusta, Georgia. I was extremely honored by this offer and asked my potential new boss to allow me to think about it for a few days. I explained to him that my mother was in assisted living in Eufaula and that I would have to think through the pros and cons of not living during the work week in the same town as she. He told me that I would not have to relocate to Georgia, and that I could operate out of a Birmingham office, which was a large concession; but still, that was three hours north of Eufaula, and I needed to really think it through.

On the upside, we did have Carol, my mother was well cared for in her current facility, and the staff loved her. Also positive was the fact that this new job would not have any supervisory or management responsibilities, but rather would be singularly focused on preparing interesting informational talks about our project and then being prepared to deliver them pretty much wherever the message needed to be taken. Although there would be significant travel involved, my new schedule would be highly flexible, far more so than with my then current assignment, and that was the biggest positive of all.

Back in 2007, just prior to returning to the plant, I had purchased and closed on a small loft apartment, with an eye toward flipping it for profit. It was situated on the twelfth floor of a beautiful granite high-rise built in 1913 and located in the smack of downtown Birmingham. The financial downturn in 2008 had proven to be the undoing of that plan, and so I had kept it. It was very convenient and comfortable and easy to keep up, and I soon realized I was relieved I had not sold it. It was an absolutely perfect place to live for access to my new office because my travel to and from was exactly opposite the heavier flow of Monday through Friday work traffic, saving me, literally, hours of downtime; plus it was only minutes from the airport.

I remembered the first day I had taken my mother to see the loft. It was totally empty, and smelled of fresh paint, its long shotgun style floor pan leading straight back to large windows overlooking the city. I can still see her, slowly walking the length of the apartment, heading to the windows to look out, the rubber tip on her thick wooden cane making little sucking noises as it made contact with the wooden floors.

During my mom's working years in downtown Birmingham in the 1950s and 60s, the structure had been known as the Comer Building, and both my mother and Aunt Gail had been in it many times before it had ever been envisioned as high-rise residential lofts.

When I talked this job offer over with Carol, she said she was more than happy to continue caring for my mother. Not only did she enjoy my mother's company, but also the extra money she earned came in handy for sure.

When I recreated through words for Mom the details of her first visit to the loft back in 2007, I shared with her that if I took this new job assignment I would be living in that apartment during the week, but would return to Eufaula on Friday afternoons to spend the weekend. I asked if she remembered being in it, and she said she did—maybe. Mom continued to show total trust in my judgment and told me to do whatever I thought was best. After some prayerful deliberation, I decided to take the job.

For the next five months, December 2009 through early May 2010, my mother fared well; and on Friday afternoons as I drove back into town, she was my first stop. Her ability to carry on conversations with me was virtually unchanged, and her ability to remember things from the past would surprise me from time to time, such as the name of the woman my father had left her for. She was still in marked discomfort with her low back. I tried heating pads set on low and back pain patches to provide relief, but her skin, thinning with age, was intolerant to both. Sometimes I would find her lying in bed, on her right-side, fully clothed, just taking the pressure of gravity off her back. I would kick off my shoes and lie next to her. Even though I was fifty years of age, it was among the most comforting feelings in the world to me.

She had developed a little habit of working the tip of her index finger against the back of her two front teeth for several minutes at a time until she got tired of holding her mouth open. I was perplexed by the habit, and one day, after vigorously washing my hands, I asked her if I could feel behind those two front teeth. She allowed it; I felt nothing alarming, figuring that the curious tongue had found a little crevice and she was using her index finger to try to figure out what it was. Trying to break her of this habit was an exercise in futility, and I would use the same expression she had used with me as a child, "Get those nasty fingers out of your mouth!" Her response was precious and child-like, jerking her finger away more quickly than I suspected she could move and then looking at me, all innocent.

On Monday morning, May 10, 2010, I left my lake house early, headed to north Georgia to give a nuclear project informational talk to a group of Rotarians. Often, if my schedule for a given Monday included a talk in a place within reasonable driving distance from Eufaula, I would cut out the Sunday afternoon return trip to Birmingham and spend Sunday night at my lake house, get up early the next morning, and be on my way. On this Monday morning, I had driven as far as Columbus, Georgia, about forty-five minutes north, when my cell phone rang. It was the administrator from my mother's assisted living facility. She calmly informed me that my mother had awakened with a deep cough, non-productive, but deep. She went on to state that she wished to err on the side of caution and have her taken to the local hospital for observation, both for my mother's sake and for the sake of the other residents in the event the cough was indicative of something contagious. I was in full agreement and told her I was in Columbus but would return as soon as possible.

I called the program organizer for the Rotarians and begged off, apologizing, but telling him I felt going back to be with my mother was the right thing to do. He was extremely gracious and said his thoughts and prayers were with us. I then called Carol and she, as usual, was a full step ahead of me and told me she would follow the ambulance to the hospital.

On my drive back to Eufaula, I thought about my visit with my mother the afternoon before. I had not noticed a cough, or even suspicioned that she didn't feel well, but I knew these things could come on rather quickly, and I was also aware of her declining ability to pinpoint discomfort and pain. About an hour later, I arrived at the small county hospital and found a parking spot. It was a beautiful spring day in the South. The fluffy white clouds looked like cotton candy stuck to the bright blue sky, and I recalled my mother's habitual notice of them. Several species of birds chirped away, singing on top of each other; and the middle-season azaleas were blooming everywhere, in bunches of white and pink and fuchsia. I hoped the news of my mother's condition would be as good as this day was beautiful.

I continued inside and asked the front desk receptionist for her room number. I consulted the signs on the wall for the series of room numbers bracketing the one housing my mother and headed off down the hallway. I found her sitting up in her bed, receiving fluids and antibiotics and looking for all the world just fine. Carol was seated in a chair beside her bed, and when I walked in they both broke into grins. I asked her how she was feeling and got her typical monosyllabic answer, "Fine." I smiled, shaking my head from side to side. I visited with her for some time, and over the course of the visit, I did hear the chesty cough that had alarmed the administrator.

The following morning I visited her again, bringing her one of her favorite breakfasts, an Egg McMuffin from McDonald's. I took heart in the fact that she still had an appetite and still had good color, and in my non-medical mind, I believed her condition was actually improving. When I visited her a little later that day and found her sitting up in bed eating a carton of orange sherbet, I was certain she was on the mend.

The on-call doctor made his rounds in the early afternoon of that Tuesday; after examining my mother, he stepped outside of her room with me and I listened intently to what he had to say. He said she was developing pneumonia and would likely never leave the hospital. I have no idea why his proclamation came as such a shock to me, but it did, and I protested, "But she looks so good." He repeated gently, "She will not leave this hospital." He then recommended that I contact Hospice.

I thanked him for his directness, and while I watched his white-coated back walk away down the long tiled hall, the words of other doctors we had seen over the last few years came back to me, "Mother has a lot going on. I recommend you not resuscitate her. She has smoker's lungs. If she ever develops pneumonia, that will be it." I knew then it was time to make some phone calls; so I telephoned Aunt Gail and told her what we were dealing with and what the doctor had said. She told me she would gather a few of "the girls" and leave Birmingham first thing Wednesday morning. I invited them to stay at my home, and my aunt said she appreciated that and would likely take me up on my offer. At that point, it was anyone's guess as to how much longer she would be with us, but the doctor had indicated only a matter of days.

My mother's bearing continued to fly in the face of the doctor's predictions. When I walked into her room mid-morning on Wednesday with Aunt Gail, Nita, and Theresa (whom we all affectionately called Teedy) in tow, she was sitting up in bed again and enjoying another carton of orange sherbet. The nurses undoubtedly knew the score, and I was extremely grateful for their compassion and thoughtfulness, allowing her as many little cartons of orange sherbet as her heart desired.

While she visited with her sister and her friends, the young female respiratory therapist came in to have a listen to Mom's lungs and then stepped away to allow the visits to continue. She then sought me out and introduced herself. I asked a few questions about how a physician determines pneumonia, and she graciously gave me the layman's answer to that question, culminating by asking me if I would like to listen to my mother's lungs with her stethoscope. I gave her a courteous but emphatic, "No, thank you." I would not risk that sound staying in my memory forever.

On Wednesday evening, my mother slipped into a coma. The Hospice volunteers helped me and Carol cover the shifts to ensure she was never alone again. Before heading home, I bent over her quiet, still body and privately whispered into her ear. I had learned that oftentimes the ability to hear is the last thing a dying patient loses, and I had to tell her, just one more time, how I felt about her. I whispered, choking back tears, "Mom, you have been the best, just the best mother a girl could hope for; and I love you with all my heart. But, Momma, if you need to go, you go. I will be okay." I sealed it with a light kiss to her temple.

Upon hearing the news that my mother had slipped into a coma, Aunt Millie, and her youngest daughter, Marygail, came straight away from Navarre, Florida, arriving in Eufaula around 5 p.m. Thursday afternoon. They drove directly to the hospital and found me, Aunt Gail, Nita, Teedy, and Carol milling about in Mother's room, talking quietly, waiting, sensing she was in her last days of life, and wondering when precisely she would decide that her earthly mission was complete.

As the supper hour approached on Thursday evening, the girls and I decided to return to my house for a quick bite to eat. Carol was there with my mother and told us to take our time. Aunt Millie and Marygail, having just recently arrived, opted to visit with Mom a while longer. Marygail had an important commitment in Navarre early the next morning; so after a good visit with Mom, she dropped Aunt Millie off at my house and returned to Navarre, completing her eight-hour round trip late into the night.

In honor of my mother, I fed the girls barbecue from Phil's with all the trimmings. We ate on the deck, also in Mom's honor, crowded around the teak table where my mother had sat just weeks before, looking out over the water.

Although already comatose by Wednesday evening, I believe with all my heart that she was waiting on three things to happen before finally letting go. First, for me to tell her that I was okay and if she needed to go, then she should go. Second, after having already seen her baby sister, I believe she waited for her middle sister to arrive, so that they could spend a few last earthly moments together. And lastly, I believe she waited for her room to be clear of family before she crossed over. Within an hour of our departure, Carol called me and told me that Mom had passed away, peacefully.

I was honored to deliver the eulogy at her funeral a few days after her death. Oddly enough, I did not cry. The sense of relief I felt for her far outweighed my own sense of loss. I knew without question she was with our Heavenly Father, out of pain, discomfort, and confusion. I concluded my tribute to my mother with this sentence: "If I am anything good in this life, it is due, in large part, to the abiding care and unconditional love of this woman." I have never uttered truer words, and remain beyond grateful to have been her daughter.

Now that she is gone, I find my everyday existence imprinted by her influence in a thousand ways. I love to eat out. I love that first sip of hot coffee in the morning. I love Tina Turner, and I love working at my desk. I find myself always searching for a name tag on my waiter and if I don't find one, I ask for their name. If the clerk gives me too much change, I return immediately to the store and give it back. I am a champion of the underdog and inflamed by injustice. I attempt to treat every living creature with dignity and respect, even if I don't like them. And I chalk up coming down on the good side of a close call to my guardian angel. Whenever I see and hear a car coming with its radio blasting too loudly, I think of the day years ago when as a teenager my mother and I saw and heard the same thing. I looked at him in disgust and shook my head from side to side. My mother looked at him with sympathy and commented, "He is just saying, 'Someone, please notice me.'" These ways and dozens of others were her ways—and have become mine.

I have tried over these many months of writing to choose a favorite from the hundreds of memories of our life together. I believe it to be this one. I am six, dressed in a simple little shift that she has cut from a pattern and sewn together with guidance from her mother. It is a dark print, in the shade our kindergarten teachers have suggested we wear for our kindergarten pictures. I am washed and scrubbed and my bangs have been freshly trimmed. I am standing just inside the front door of our home in Birmingham, about to go outside to join my father in the car for the trek to school. She bends down so that we are face to face and tells me how nice I look. I can smell the spicy sweet Jergens lotion on her beautiful soft hands and watch, a little cross-eyed, as she gently licks both of her thumbs and, starting just above the bridge of my nose, makes opposing sweeping arcs, settling my eyebrows into orderly lines. Then, with a kiss and an "I love you," she tells me to be a good girl and sends me out—emblematic of our fifty years together.

Thank you for allowing me to share her story.

—The End—